The Artful Home™

Furniture, Sculpture & Objects

A Source & Guide for Living with Art

The Artful Home ™

Furniture, Sculpture & Objects

A Source & Guide for Living with Art

Louis Sagar, Executive Editor

GUILD Publishing
Madison, Wisconsin

The ArtfulHome™

Furniture, Sculpture & Objects

A Source & Guide for Living with Art

Louis Sagar, Executive Editor

PUBLISHER

GUILD Sourcebooks
An imprint of GUILD, LLC
931 E. Main Street
Madison, Wisconsin 53703
TEL 608-257-2590 • TEL 877-284-8453

ADMINISTRATION

Toni Sikes, CEO and Founder
Reed McMillan, Vice President of Sales
Jeanne Gohlke, Administrative Assistant

DESIGN, PRODUCTION AND EDITORIAL

Georgene Pomplun, Art Director
Sue Englund, Production Artist
Katie Kazan, Chief Editorial Officer
Jill Schaefer, Editorial/Production Coordinator
Jori Finkel and Susan Troller, Writers (Artist Profiles)

ARTIST CONSULTANTS

Nicole Carroll • Carla Dillman • Lori Dumm
Amy Lambright • Laura Marth • Mike Mitchell

Copyright © 2003 GUILD, LLC
ISBN 1-880140-50-0

Printed in China

Cover art: Interior design by Mary Drysdale. Photograph: Andrew Lautman. Also shown on page 1.
Page 2: Interior design by Mary Drysdale. Photograph: Andrew Lautman. See pages 96-97.
Page 3: Anahata Arts, *Exposed Heart*, mixed-media sculpture. Photograph: Eric Gutelewitz. See page 213.
Opposite: Philip Sollman, cherry and white oak dining set. See page 27.

GUILD.com is the Internet's leading retailer of original art and fine craft. Visit www.guild.com.

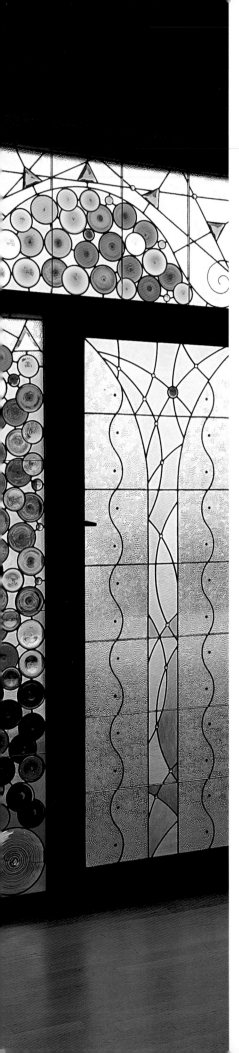

TABLE OF CONTENTS

Introduction

Articles and Tips

THE ROOMS OF YOUR HOME

TIPS FOR AN ARTFUL HOME

❧

The Artful Home shows artwork of enduring value; we think you'll refer to it for years
to come. If, at any time, you're not able to reach an artist through contact information
included in this book, call GUILD at 1-877-284-8453. We keep track of updated
phone numbers and the like, and are glad to share our most current information.

❧

Left: Larry Zgoda, untitled glass entry (detail). Photograph: Richard Bruck. See page 108.

TABLE OF CONTENTS

Artist Display Pages

Representative work from *Artful Home* artists, organized by discipline and complete with
addresses and phone numbers so you can contact artists directly for special projects and purchases.

Artists Profiles

Resources

WELCOME TO THE ARTFUL HOME

When GUILD asked me to become the executive editor for a series of books titled *The Artful Home*, I turned to my friends. What did they think about the proposed series? How did they feel about buying art? Owning art? Living with art?

These questions elicited interesting responses. As I'd suspected, many people feel intimidated by art and by artists. The idea of going to a museum or gallery and looking at art makes some of my friends feel insecure. Some feel a sense of exclusion, or say that galleries are cold and uninviting. Another common complaint: people think there's an elusive "right" way to look at art, but they aren't sure what it is. Several of my close friends feel it's all a big mystery, as if enjoying art requires membership in an elite club, a club they have not been invited to join.

Even those who consider themselves art collectors mentioned that the buying process is sometimes confusing. How are values established? Why are some pieces so expensive and others so modest in cost?

It didn't take long for me to realize how common these feelings and questions are. In fact, there is no right or wrong way to look at art. The goal is to follow your own instincts, make your own choices and learn how to live with art that you love. And although many factors influence price and value, our most important goal should be to develop, and then refine, an individual approach to looking at and enjoying the art we acquire and display in our homes. From there, all other considerations, including value and pricing, will fall easily into place.

This book offers insights and strategies for achieving that goal. It also answers questions that have surfaced over the course of researching this book—questions about commissioning custom-designed artwork, about caring for art of various mediums and about displaying art in your home. The book you're holding now, *Furniture, Sculpture & Objects*, is one of two volumes in the *Artful Home* series. The companion volume, *Art for the Wall*, focuses on murals; tile; trompe l'oeil finishes and works in fiber, glass and other craft media, as well as paintings, prints and photographs. Both volumes are available directly from GUILD Publishing (1-877-344-8453 or www.guild.com).

Appreciating original art and finding ways to bring art into your home are both central to the journey and the focus of this book. It's one thing to realize that a particular work of art is inspiring and pleasurable to you. It's another to determine whether a sculpture you've taken a fancy to will actually fit in with everything else going on in your living room, or whether a handmade rocking chair will coexist happily with the dining room furniture you inherited from your grandparents.

Our homes provide a wonderful context in which to display art and nurture our own creativity. *The Artful Home* volumes, filled as they are with suggestions, information and practical tips, are designed to help demystify artists and their work. Each volume includes artist profiles; tips about selecting, caring for and living with art; photographs of homes enriched by art; a glossary of terms and definitions; and a list of terrific galleries.

These books are part guide and part sourcebook. The artists included in each volume have works available for purchase from their studios. They are also available for custom projects—commissioned works of art that fit, hand-to-glove, into the styles, spaces and colors of your home. Whether by phone or e-mail, these artists want to hear from you.

One of my most important goals as editor and guide for this series of books is to suggest a point of view about creating an artful home. It begins with a philosophy of sorts; turn to page 12 to see what I mean. Once understood, this philosophy will empower you to learn about art and artists at your own pace and in your own way. As you'll see, there is pure pleasure to be gained when we immerse ourselves in the process.

Let's get started.

— Louis Sagar, Executive Editor

Gold gilding and cream fabrics connect traditional with contemporary in these two chairs, which complement the light walls and hearth while contrasting elegantly with the rich black of the wall piece and table. A Mary Drysdale design. Photograph: Andrew Lautman.

HOW TO USE *THE ARTFUL HOME*
Your Direct Connection to Artists' Studios

The decision to live with art is a decision to live with things of enduring value. The paintings, prints and photographs you place in your home—like the works of art in clay, fiber, metal, glass and wood—enrich your life with a silent and strengthening presence, and with the joy of beauty and imagination.

Because original art can be costly compared to manufactured goods, and because each artwork is unique, shopping for art calls for research and initiative. Hence *The Artful Home*. Two companion volumes invite you to browse, buy and commission works of art directly from the studios of exceptional contemporary artists.

> *Art for the Wall* features paintings, photographs, prints, art quilts, tapestries and works for the wall in fiber, paper, ceramics, glass, metal and mixed media.

> *Furniture, Sculpture & Objects* features furniture, lighting, floor coverings, architectural details and art objects in all media, as well as sculpture for pedestals and gardens.

Full-color photographs make it easy to find the artists whose style appeals to you most, while complete contact information allows you to get in touch with those artists directly to purchase existing pieces or commission custom-designed works.

You need not be an art collector to purchase works from artists included in *The Artful Home*. In fact, the only qualifications you really need are a sincere appreciation for the artists you call and a genuine interest in owning their work.

10

FINDING WHAT YOU NEED
A Roadmap to The Artful Home

Want to contact an artist featured in *The Artful Home?* Look for addresses, phone numbers and other contact information at the tops of artists' display pages. Additional information about each artist can be found in the Artist Information section in the back of the book; listings are in alphabetical order by the heading on each artist's page. This is where you'll find information about the artists' mediums and techniques, their range of products and their notable awards or commissions.

If you know what type of artwork you want to purchase or commission, a search by section will help you find results quickly. You'll find a list of sections in the Table of Contents. Likewise, if you know the name of the artist you want to work with, you can easily search using the Index of Artists and Companies, found in the back of the book. If you would like to work with an artist in your area, check the Geographic Index, which lists artists by location.

Curious to know more about an artist's work? Don't hesitate to contact them directly; they'll be delighted to hear from you. And for more information about these and other artists who create works for home environments, visit the GUILD Custom Design Center, a featured service of GUILD.com.

Opposite: Lynn Basa, *Formation*, wool rug. Photograph: Russell Johnson.

PUTTING THE BOOK TO WORK

We welcome you to browse *The Artful Home,* enjoying the artwork, the artist profiles and the many suggestions for building a home rich in beauty and creative energy. But there's more to this book than that. Every one of our featured artists invites you to call or e-mail to purchase pieces from their studio or to arrange a commission for a custom work of art.

Your call to an *Artful Home* artist can take you in many directions.

- The same artworks shown on these pages may be available for immediate purchase. Some of these works are from an artist's production line or created in limited editions; others are one-of-a-kind pieces.

- The artist may have other available works on hand. If you live near the artist (see the Geographic Index), consider visiting the studio. If a studio visit isn't feasible, ask to see images; these can often be e-mailed for quick review.

- Alternately, you could hire the artist to create a unique work that reflects your home, your aesthetic and, perhaps, some landmark event in your life or the life of someone you love. For help in commissioning artworks, consider the services of GUILD's Custom Design Center. You can reach the CDC from GUILD's home page (www.guild.com), or call CDC staff at 1-877-344-8453.

When viewing an artist's page, keep in mind that while the projects shown are representative of the artist's work, they don't demonstrate the full extent of the artist's capabilities. If you like a certain style but want something other than the works pictured here, call the artist and talk it over. He or she may be intrigued at the prospect of exploring new forms.

HOME AS SANCTUARY

Home is the one place in our lives that is uniquely ours. It is a space that reflects where we come from, who we are and how we got here.

I often think of my home as a white canvas; the rooms are empty and the spaces are filled with natural light. I do this mental exercise because, in reality, my home is like yours: not perfect. Kids, cats, too much clutter, stuff to throw away. Just dreaming about empty space and soft lighting puts me in a better mood.

Like an artist, I use a set of tools to create within my white canvas. My tools include a favorite set of markers, a scrapbook for clippings and a diary for recording flashes of insight. I have a big imagination and like to change my mind a lot, and these tools help me develop my aesthetic on paper, where it's easy to try different options. They help me know what I like.

A personal aesthetic develops from building a point of view about space, proportions and texture. I find that I can identify and refine that point of view by using the markers, scrapbook and diary to identify colors, patterns and types of art that are meaningful to me. This exercise takes practice and matures over time, but once I find the aesthetic values that are meaningful to me—and develop those values in the design and content of my home—I have something wonderful to share with family and friends. The process of sharing feels comforting, and comfort is one of my key goals. Over the years, I've found that home is the sanctuary where I can accomplish that goal.

Artist Bennett Bean in his artful home.
See page 124. Photograph: A. Hufnagel.

From a historical perspective, we've only recently had the time to look at our homes as more than shelter from nature and the elements. The daily activities of cleaning, maintaining and repairing are an essential part of homemaking. Shopping for furnishings and decorating are other parts of the rhythm. Arranging flowers, playing music and lighting candles all combine to create an atmosphere that stimulates the senses and sets the mood.

I like to think of the entire homemaking process as a journey, one without beginning or end, limited only by my time and imagination.

As you become more artful in your approach to your home, slow down and enjoy the process of getting there. In a world where so much is result-driven, projects at home need not be rushed. Take time to visualize home spaces that are new and refreshing. Take time to look at art and to think about the kinds of artworks you want to live with. Learn about the artists whose work speaks to you, about their inspirations and their techniques. This knowledge enables you to train your eyes and enriches your personal aesthetic. It helps strengthen your point of view and it helps you define who you are.

So when you think about your home, think like an artist.

—L.S.

ART FOR YOUR HOME'S DISTINCTIVE SPACES

Rooms are the energy centers of your home. They vibrate with an ebb and flow that change with the time of day and time of year.

In creating an artful home, your goal is to establish a thematic point of view for each room in your house. Your challenge is to balance the functional needs of the room with a story that expresses something about you—your tastes, your values, your heritage. The color palette, the style and arrangement of your furnishings, the art that you live with—all help to tell your story.

Few rooms in a home function solely in the traditional roles suggested by their names. Most serve multiple functions, and this flexibility presents opportunities for a personalized and creative approach to decorating. Once again, art can play an important role. The selection and placement of the art you own is a powerful way to communicate something about your soul, about who you are at the core of your being.

Above: Diana Harrison, *Poppy Lamps* (left) and *Three Irisis in a Pot*, table lamp. Photograph: John Harkey. See pages 83, 87 and 202.

14

Glass, metal and wood are wonderfully interwoven and balanced in this utilitarian interior design by Mary Drysdale. Notice how the arrangement of the artwork and the soft lighting immediately invite the viewer's eye up the stairs and into the home. Photograph: Andrew Lautman. Photograph of Mary Drysdale, opposite page: Mary Noble Ours.

A CONVERSATION WITH
MARY DOUGLAS DRYSDALE

Mary Douglas Drysdale is one of the premier interior designers in North America today. Examples of her designs appear throughout this book and on the book's cover. These interior spaces resonate with taste and style, each one a distinctive integration of her three passions: art, architecture and decoration.

A Mary Drysdale design is strongly anchored in classical themes; at the same time, it intimately reveals the interests and personalities of her clients. This kind of synthesis is made possible by her keen capacity to listen and interpret.

"After all," she says, "designing is a collaborative process. I think of my role largely as that of guide and teacher; I make sure the client is involved in the process. By contrast, the conventional role of the client is simply to delegate, leaving the decisions to the designer. In these instances, more often than not, you end up with a house—not a home.

"When I begin a project, I focus on helping clients get in touch with styles they like and styles they don't. I encourage them to express themselves and make special note of their passions. In every project, I'm challenged to integrate the personal imprint of the client with a harmonious and balanced interior.

"We all have an inherent talent to express ourselves in the sanctuary of our own homes. It is the role of the designer to facilitate that expression, so that the home becomes a reflection of self and can evolve over time."

MARY DRYSDALE'S KEYS TO AN ARTFUL HOME

- 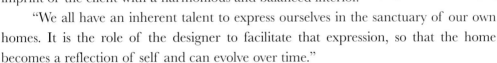 Interior designing is like art directing. Create a visual composition in each room and establish points of continuity between rooms. Think of your furnishings, objects and framed artworks as elements in an ever-changing still life.
- Evaluate the open spaces in each room. These literal and visual pathways need space to breathe; don't let them suffocate from too much stuff! Put it away, give it away or throw it away.
- In the end, good interior design tells a story. Great interior design tells a story about you.

COMMISSIONING A WORK OF ART

There's something exhilarating about engaging an artist to create a unique work of art for your home. Custom-designed (or "commissioned") works of art reflect your personal taste and vision more deeply than "off-the-shelf" artworks. At the same time, they can significantly enhance the value of your home.

Commissioned works of art may or may not be expensive, depending upon the scope of the project, but they will always require your personal involvement. If you enjoy that involvement, art commissions are the ultimate way to buy original art. Custom-designed artworks—whether freestanding, as with a sculpture or dining room table, or structurally integrated, as with a wrought iron garden gate—can become instant family treasures, adding deeply to the heritage of who you are.

CHOOSING AN ARTIST

The most important step you'll take when planning a commission is the choice of artist. Who is the right choice? Someone whose previous art projects appeal to you. Whose previous clients are enthusiastic. Who has undertaken similar projects in the past and delivered completed work within the agreed-upon budget and schedule.

And how do you find this individual?

The Artful Home is a wonderful place to start. Every one of our featured artists accepts commissions for custom-designed artwork, and the contact information included with their individual display pages will put you in touch with them directly. You may also want to talk with friends who have hired artists for commissions similar to yours, or visit artists' studios and art fairs to talk with possible candidates in person.

16

Above: Earth Fire Designs, fireplaces. See page 95.

Once your A-list is narrowed down to two or three names, it's time to schedule meetings to discuss the project, either face-to-face (for local artists) or by phone. As you talk, try to determine the artist's interest in your project, and pay attention to your own comfort level with the artist. Try to find out whether the chemistry is right—whether you have the basis to build a working relationship—and confirm that the artist has the necessary skills to undertake your project. Be thorough and specific when asking questions. Is the artist excited about the project? What does he or she see as the most important issues or considerations? Will your needs be a major or minor concern? Evaluate the artist's style, approach and personality.

If it feels like you might have trouble working together, take heed. But if all goes well and it feels like a good fit, ask for a list of references. These are important testimonials, so don't neglect to make the calls. Ask about the artist's work habits and communication style, and—of course—about the success of the artwork. You should also ask whether the project was delivered on time and within budget. If you like what you hear, you'll be one important step closer to hiring your artist.

Expect Professionalism

Once you've selected the artist, careful planning and communication can help ensure a great outcome. If this is an expensive or complicated project, you may want to request preliminary designs at this time. Since most artists charge a design fee whether or not they're ultimately hired for the project, start by asking for sketches from your top candidate. If you're unhappy with the designs submitted, you can go to your second choice. If, on the other hand, the design is what you'd hoped for, it's time to finalize your working agreement with this artist.

17

Left: Mollie Massie, *Leafing Out* fire screen. Photograph: Rob Melnychuk. See page 71. Right: Elizabeth MacDonald, Hubbard tile fireplace surround. Photograph: Bob Rush.

As you discuss contract details, be resolved that silence is not golden and ignorance is not bliss! Be frank. Discuss the budget and timetable, and be sure that these and other important details are spelled out in the contract. Now is the time for possible misunderstandings to be brought up and resolved—not later, when the work is half done and deadlines loom.

THE CONTRACT: PUTTING IT IN WRITING

It's a truism in any kind of business that it's always cheaper to get the lawyers involved at the beginning of a process than after something goes wrong. In the case of custom-made works of art, a signed contract or letter of agreement commits the artist to completing his or her work on time and to specifications. It also assures the artist that he or she will get paid the right amount at the right time. That just about eliminates the biggest conflicts that can arise.

Contracts should be specific to the job. If your commission is for holiday ornaments bearing your company's logo, a sales slip noting down payment and delivery date should do the trick. If, on the other hand, you've hired a cabinetmaker to build and install glass-fronted bookshelves for the living room in your new home, a more detailed document will be needed.

Customarily, artists are responsible for design, production, shipping and installation. If someone else is to be responsible for installation, be sure you specify who will coordinate and pay for it. With a large project, it's helpful to identify the tasks that, if delayed for any reason, would set back completion of the project. These should be discussed up front to assure that both parties agree on requirements and expectations.

Above: Nancy Smith Klos, *Healing Trilogy*, tapestry. Photograph: Charlie Kloppenberg.

Payment Schedule

The more skill you need and the more complex the project, the more you should budget for the artist's work and services. With larger projects, payments are usually tied to specific milestones; these serve as checkpoints and assure that work is progressing in a satisfactory manner, on time and on budget. Payment is customarily made in three stages, although—again—this will depend on the circumstances, scope and complexity of the project.

The first payment for a large-scale commission is usually made when the contract is signed. It covers the artist's time and creativity in developing a detailed design specific to your needs. For larger projects, you can expect to go through several rounds of trial and error in the design process, but at the end of this stage you'll have detailed drawings and, for three-dimensional work, an approved maquette (model). The cost of the maquette and the design time are usually factored into the artist's fee.

The second payment is generally set for a point midway through the project and is for work completed to date. If the materials are expensive, the artist may also ask that you advance money at this stage to cover their costs. If the commission is canceled during this period, the artist keeps the money already paid for work performed.

Final payment is usually due when the work is finished or, if so arranged, installed. Sometimes the artwork is finished on time but the building is delayed (as so often happens with new construction); in this case, the artist should be paid upon completion but still has the obligation to oversee installation.

WHERE TO FIND HELP

If your project is large and expensive, or if it needs to be carefully coordinated with other aesthetic and functional aspects of your home, consider hiring an art consultant. The consultant can help with complicated contract arrangements and make certain that communication between the artist and professionals such as architects, interior designers and engineers is clear and complete.

Another terrific service is available online through GUILD, the publisher of *The Artful Home*. The GUILD Custom Design Center lets you describe special projects by filling out an online form. Your information is shared with qualified artists over the Internet; GUILD then forwards their proposals to you. This is a great way to find artists when you're celebrating a family milestone, solving a design problem or looking for ways to make everyday objects artful.

One thing to keep in mind: some people may feel that the process of commissioning a work of art for the home involves a degree of involvement that they just don't want to take on. If that describes you, rest assured—you may still find that treasured work of art! Most artists have a wide selection of completed works on hand in their studios, giving you the option to purchase something that's ready-made. If you find something great among the artist's inventory, don't hesitate to buy it. The piece you choose will still be unique, and it will still reflect your personal aesthetic sense. Your goal should be to develop an individual approach to enjoying art … and that includes your comfort level with how you purchase it.

FURNITURE

ROBERT CALDWELL, DESIGNER/CRAFTSMAN

ROBERT CALDWELL ■ PO BOX 407 ■ BROWNSBORO, TX 75756 ■ TEL 903-360-7305
E-MAIL RCDESIGN@FLASH.NET ■ WWW.RCALDWELLDESIGN.COM

Top left: *Arts and Crafts Chair #1*, 1999, cherry, wenge and leather with oil finish, 35" × 17" × 19". Top right: *Chinese Tables*, 2001, African mahogany with oil finish, 24" × 18" × 18" and 30" × 18" × 18". Bottom right: *Bentwood Chair*, 2000, mahogany with oil finish, 35" × 22" × 20". Bottom left: *Yin Yang Table*, 2000, walnut and padauk with laquer finish, 24" × 18" Dia. Photographs: Robert Langham.

MICHAEL T. MAXWELL

M. T. MAXWELL FURNITURE COMPANY ■ 715 MAXWELL CIRCLE ■ BEDFORD, VA 24523
TEL 1-800-686-1844 ■ E-MAIL MTMAXWELL@AOL.COM ■ WWW.MAXWELLFURNITURE.COM

Top: 2-cushion and 3-cushion settles, cherry with walnut accents and black leather cushions, 2-cushion: 25"H x 57.5"L x 37"D, 3-cushion: 25"H x 81.5"L x 37"D.
Bottom: Trestle table with trestle bench and Anne Maxwell side chairs, cherry with walnut accents, table: 30"H x 42"W x 72"L,
bench: 33"H x 18"W x 64"L, side chairs: 44"H x 21"W x 18"D. Photographs: Jill Markwood, Markwood Photography.

JOHN CLARK

JOHN CLARK FURNITURE ■ PO BOX 36 ■ PENLAND, NC 28765
TEL 828-765-5785 ■ FAX 828-765-7510 ■ E-MAIL JOHN@MAIN.NC.US

24

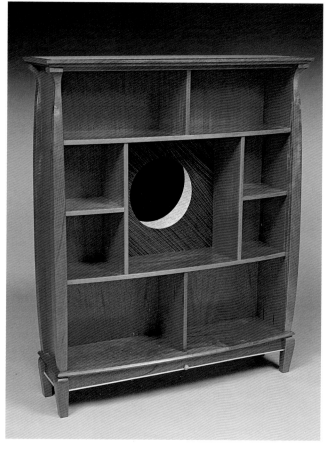

Top left: *Moon Dining Table* and chairs, mahogany and quilted maple, seats 12. Photograph: Robert Cutter.
Top right: *Moon Table*, mahogany and rosewood, 48" Dia. Photograph: Tim Barnwell. Bottom right: *Legal Bookcase*, mahogany and curly maple, 84" x 48" x 18".
Photograph: Gil Ford. Bottom left: *Moon Bookcase*, mahogany, maple and rosewood, 56" x 48" x 12". Photograph: Tim Barnwell.

RON BENOIT

WOODENSOUND FINE WOODWORKING ▨ 1613 EAST 800 SOUTH ▨ PRESTON, ID 83263 ▨ TEL 208-852-3543
E-MAIL WOODENSOUND@GEMSTATE.NET ▨ WWW.WOODENSOUND.COM

Left: *Sunburst* armoire, 2001, mahogany, South American rosewood and cedar, 75" × 48" × 26".
Top right: *Wizards'* chess table, 2002, mahogany with inlays of ebony and curly maple, 30" × 36". Bottom right: *Sunburst* demilune, 2001, quilted maple and purpleheart, 30" × 40" × 21".

BOSTWICK DESIGNS

TERRY BOSTWICK ■ 22985 BLAND CIRCLE ■ WEST LINN, OR 97068 ■ TEL 503-657-7489 ■ FAX 503-657-7950
E-MAIL NVO21@AOL.COM ■ WWW.TERRYBOSTWICKSTUDIO.COM

26

Top: Console with mirror, 2000, Douka mahogany veneer, Honduran mahogany and patinated steel, 72" x 78" x 20". Photograph: Harold Wood.
Bottom right: White sculpture stand, 2002, bleached eastern maple and curly maple veneer, 29" x 17" x 17". Photograph: Mark Stein.
Bottom left: Side chair, cherry and upholstery. Photograph: Jon Jensen.

PHILIP S. SOLLMAN

STEVENS-SOLLMAN STUDIOS ▓ 318 NORTH FILLMORE ROAD ▓ BELLEFONTE, PA 16823
TEL 814-355-3332 ▓ E-MAIL STEVSOLLMN@AOL.COM

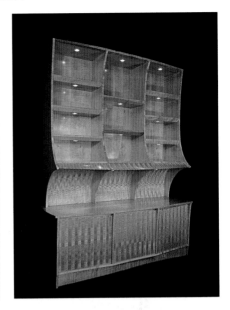

Top left: Dining chair, cherry and white oak, 24" x 24" x 40". Top center: Rocker, walnut and white oak, 42" x 28" x 46". Top right: Display unit, tiger maple, 72" x 24" x 96".
Bottom: Dining set, cherry and white oak, table dimensions: 84" x 48" x 28".

JOHN WESLEY WILLIAMS

WILLIAMS FURNITURE DESIGN ▦ PO BOX 1157 ▦ LEWISBURG, WV 24901 ▦ TEL 304-645-7579
E-MAIL JWILLIAMS@STARGATE.NET ▦ WWW.JOHNWESLEYWILLIAMSFURNITURE.COM

Left: Tall case of drawers, birdseye maple and padauk, 84" × 36" × 36", limited edition. Photograph: Jim Osborn.
Top right: Carved sideboard, birdseye maple and curly maple, 36" × 56" × 20". Photograph: Mike Keller.
Bottom right: *Boston Desk and Chair*, 2001, birdseye maple and ebony, 35" × 72" × 26", limited edition. Photograph: Jim Osborn.

BRAD SMITH

BRADFORD WOODWORKING ▨ 3120 FISHER ROAD BOX 157 ▨ WORCESTER, PA 19490 ▨ TEL 610-584-1150 ▨ FAX 610-584-1223
E-MAIL BRAD@BRADFORDWOODWORKING.COM ▨ WWW.BRADFORDWOODWORKING.COM

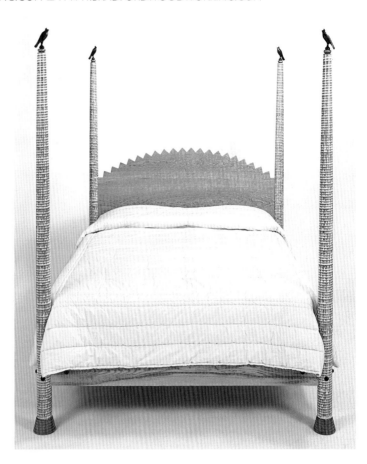

29

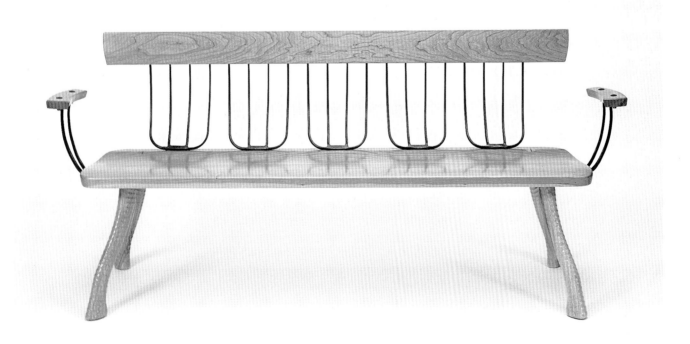

Top left: *Chest of Drawers*, hickory, sycamore, red oak, white oak, elm, maple, ash, walnut and salvaged lumber, 48" × 24" × 19". Top right: *Highpost Bed*, cherry, ash and steel, queen size, 88"H. Bottom: *Pitchfork Bench (Five Forker)*, cherry, ash and steel, 32" × 74" × 23". Photographs: Michael O'Neill.

RIVERSIDE ARTISANS

JAMES GALILEO ▦ 176 EAST 7TH STREET ▦ PATERSON, NJ 07524 ▦ TEL 973-278-5881
E-MAIL RIVERSIDEARTISANS@WORLDNET.ATT.NET

30

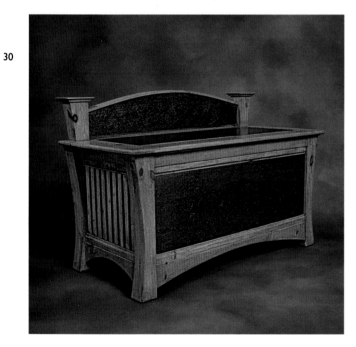

Top left: *Fellinger* table, 1998, mahogany, crotch mahogany and satinwood, 53" x 34" x 25".
Top right: *Jo Jo* bench, 2001, figured maple, 42" x 35" x 20". Bottom right: *Demi-lune* hall table, 2002, mahogany, crotch mahogany and pomele sapele, 42" x 36" x 14".
Bottom left: Chest, 1999, eastern pine and copper paint, 36" x 24" x 16". Photographs: Bob Skinner.

ZUERNER DESIGN LLC

PETER F. ZUERNER ■ 825 WEST MAIN ROAD ■ MIDDLETOWN, RI 02842 ■ TEL 401-846-9490 ■ FAX 401-846-9470
E-MAIL INFO@ZUERNERDESIGN.COM ■ WWW.ZUERNERDESIGN.COM

Top: *Sit Around Chair,* 2001, cherry and chenille fabric, 30"H x 24"W x 24"D. Bottom: *Hope St. Media Cabinet,* 2002, cherry and cocobolo (custom sized). Photographs: Lauren Page.

32

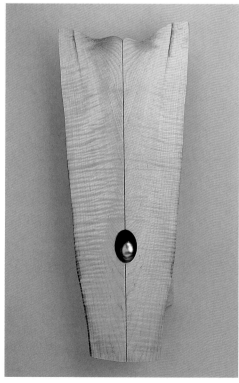

Top: *Canyon* series coffee table, 2000, curly Swiss pear and ebonized cherry, 18" x 58" x 31.5". Bottom right: *Mariposa IV* wall cabinet, spalted maple, ebonized cherry and dyed birdseye maple, 28.5" x 19" x 5". Bottom left: *Ovum* wall cabinet, curly maple, dyed curly maple and gilded egg, 31.5" x 14" x 4". Photographs: John Polak.

ANDREW MUGGLETON

E-MAIL DESIGNS@ANDREWMUGGLETON.COM ■ WWW.ANDREWMUGGLETON.COM

Top: *Tall Curved Drawers*, bird's-eye maple, wenge, frosted glass and aluminum, 60" × 23" × 22".
Bottom: *Lotus Bench*, bird's-eye maple, wenge and ultrasuede, 31" × 71" × 23". Photographs: Patrick Minniear.

PETER PIEROBON

121 EAST FIRST STREET ■ NORTH VANCOUVER, BC V7L 1B2 ■ CANADA ■ TEL 604-984-6446
E-MAIL PIEROBON3@AOL.COM

34

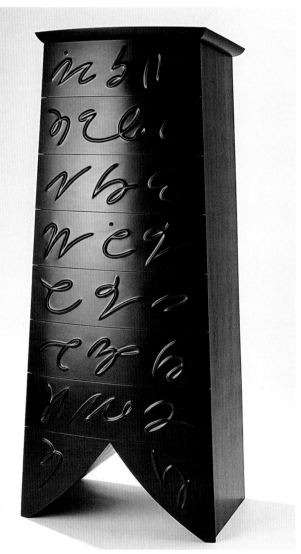

Top left: *Mariners*, ebonized mahogany pedestals, 40"H × 36"W × 20"D.
Top right: Writing desk, leather, ebony and mahogany, 30"H × 86"W × 36"D. Bottom right: *Jargon*, ebonized mahogany chest, 71"H × 31"W × 26"D.
Bottom left: *Book Knowledge*, mahogany and bronze, 80"H × 50"W × 28"D. Photographs: Tom Brummett.

DEAN PULVER

PO BOX 1457 ■ EL PRADO, NM 87529 ■ TEL 505-751-4402
E-MAIL DEAN@DEANPULVER.COM ■ WWW.DEANPULVER.COM

Top: Entertainment center, 2002, walnut and aniline dye, 36" x 112" x 26". Right: Wardrobe, 2002, walnut and aniline dye, 108" x 60" x 24". Bottom left: *My Friend's Friend*, 2002, walnut and aniline dye, 30" x 27" x 22". Center left: *My Friend* dining chair, 2001, walnut and aniline dye, 32" x 27" x 26". Photographs: Pat Pollard.

JENNA GOLDBERG

75 WILLOW STREET UNIT C ▪ PROVIDENCE, RI 02909 ▪ TEL 401-339-1448 ▪ FAX 401-454-0233
E-MAIL JENNA43215@MINDSPRING.COM ▪ WWW.JENNAGOLDBERGSTUDIO.COM

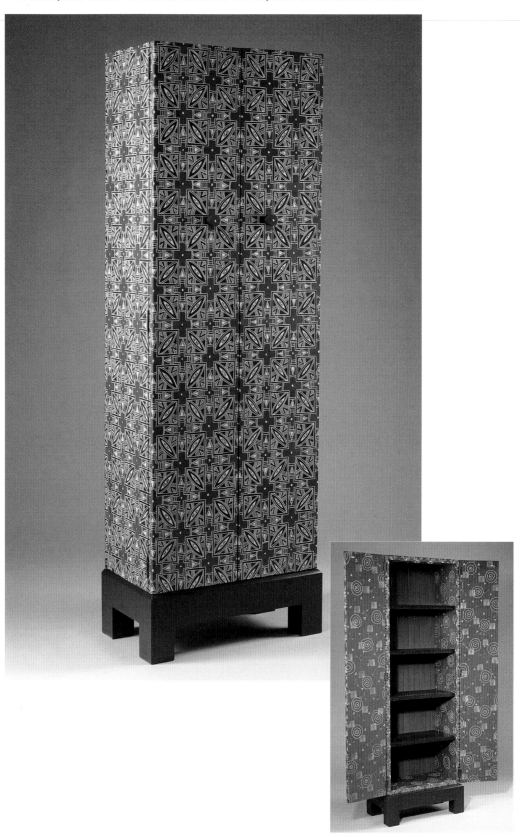

36

Dragonfly cabinet, 2002, carved and painted basswood, 24" x 14" x 70". Inset: *Dragonfly cabinent* (open). Photograph: Mark Johnston.

A WORD ABOUT FENG SHUI

Feng shui (pronounced *fung shwey*) is an ancient Chinese discipline dedicated to the study of energy, or *chi*, as it relates to movement and pattern in physical environments. Feng shui provides insight into how our environments affect our physical, emotional and spiritual well-being. The principles of classical feng shui were closely guarded in ancient China. The keepers of this secret knowledge were the feng shui masters, highly respected scientists and astronomers who were responsible for sustaining the good health, prosperity and power of the imperial dynasties.

The practice of feng shui enlightens, harmonizes and improves lives by identifying the natural rhythms of energy that affect us daily. A basic understanding of feng shui can help you promote positive energy flow in each room of your home and throughout your household. This understanding can influence your selection and placement of artworks.

A host of books about feng shui are available. Here are some favorites: *A Master Course in Feng Shui* by Eva Wong (Shambhala Publications); *The Feng Shui Journal: A Guided Workbook to Bring Harmony Into Your Life* by Teresa Polanco and Chris Paschke (Peter Pauper Press); *Feng Shui in 10 Simple Lessons* by Jane Butler-Biggs (Watson-Guptill Press).

Vertical plays against horizontal in this wonderful arrangement by Mary Drysdale. Notice how the pattern created in the back of the chair echoes the placement of the two wall pieces over the table. Photograph: Jeannie O'Donnel.

JONATHAN BENSON

JONATHAN BENSON FURNITURE ▧ 104 HAOZOUS ROAD ▧ SANTA FE, NM 87508 ▧ TEL 505-473-9172 ▧ FAX 505-473-9109
E-MAIL JON@BENSONFURNITURE.COM ▧ WWW.BENSONFURNITURE.COM

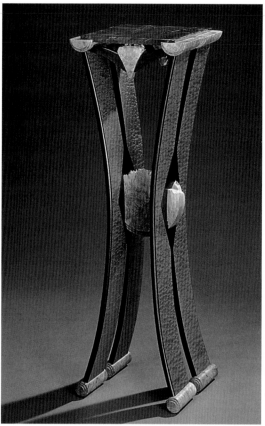

Top left: Tilt-top dictionary stand, cherry and maple burl, 40" x 18" x 16". Top right: Pedestal, pommele sapele, maple burl and marble top, 43" x 15" x 14". Bottom: *Desert Sun* buffet, vintage Brazilian rosewood, curly maple and Macassar ebony, 36" x 72" x 20". Photographs: James Hart.

KINOE KOMODA DESIGNS

KINOE KOMODA ▪ 4565 ALICE STREET ▪ SAN DIEGO, CA 92115 ▪ TEL 619-582-3717 ▪ FAX 619-583-8224
E-MAIL KINOEKOMODA@AOL.COM

39

Top: *Shibui Cheerio*, 2001, polychromed mahogany and mixed media, 8" × 60" × 6".
Bottom: Bench, from the *Kyoto* series, polychromed mahogany, 18" × 72" × 22". Photographs: Michael James Studio.

SCOTT GROVE

CONCEPT GROVE INC. ▦ 19 SWEET VERNAL COURT ▦ ROCHESTER, NY 14623 ▦ TEL/FAX 585-334-1232
E-MAIL SCOTT@SCOTTGROVE.COM ▦ WWW.SCOTTGROVE.COM

Top: *Jane* buffet, 2000, lacewood, copper leaf and copper polychrome finish, 72" × 30" × 19.5". Photograph: David Mohney Studio.
Bottom: *Eidelbaub Sr.* accent display table, 2001, pommele sapele, ebonized oak, composite, copper polychrome finish, 84" × 36" × 11".

DAVID CODDAIRE

755 EAST 10TH STREET ■ OAKLAND, CA 94606 ■ TEL 510-451-7353 ■ FAX 510-451-7351
E-MAIL TALLIRONVASES@MINDSPRING.COM

Top left: *Wavy Cabinet*, 60" × 24", steel with transparent epoxy dye. Top right: *Widemouth Vase*, 30" × 24", steel with transparent epoxy dye.
Bottom left: *Walk-up Vanity*, 60" × 24" × 14", steel with transparent epoxy dye. Bottom right: *Spiral Stool*, 18" × 18", steel with transparent epoxy dye.

ERIK A. WOLKEN

WORKS IN WOOD ▪ 3315-C HIGHWAY 54 WEST ▪ CHAPEL HILL, NC 27516
TEL 919-932-1873 ▪ E-MAIL EWOLKEN@MINDSPRING.COM

Top: Chairs, 2002, mahogany, ash and paint.
Bottom: *Table for my Tribe*, 1998, maple and poplar; 30" x 82" x 41". Photographs: Seth Tice-Lewis.

CINDY VARGAS

493 SOUTH EUCLID AVENUE #4 ▨ PASADENA, CA 91101 ▨ TEL 626-676-7841
E-MAIL CVARGASFURNITURE@CS.COM ▨ WWW.CINDYVARGASFURNITURE.COM

Top left: Chest with silk façade, 1999, mahogany and hand-dyed silk, 40" × 45" × 15". Photograph: Matt Siber.
Right: Carved chest, 2002, mahogany, 69.5" × 29.75" × 16.6". Photograph: Susan Strayer.
Bottom left: *Autumn Comes Early*, 1999, birch, milkpaint and hand-dyed silk, 52" × 31" × 15.5". Photograph: Matt Siber.

TALKING TO THE ARTIST
Jamie Robertson

"I don't like brown furniture," says Jamie Robertson, who runs little risk of being grouped with the monochromatic crowd. With more than 30 years of experience making furniture in the Boston area, Robertson rests his reputation on cleanly designed pieces that make use of richly colored woods and highly imaginative carvings.

"From the start, I've used furniture as a sort of a vehicle for decoration," says the artist, who began working in wood in the early 1970s. Robertson refined his woodworking techniques both on his own and as part of the Cambridgeport Cooperative Woodshop (1973–1990), which he helped to found. The members of the co-op often shared projects, tools, wages and ideas.

Today one of Robertson's specialties is marquetry, the art of cutting and fitting together fine strips of wood, known as veneers, to create a single surface. He calls it the ultimate jigsaw puzzle. "I use veneers because I love their variety, the different effects I can create, the color combinations," says Robertson.

Given this attention to color, it's no surprise that Robertson is a fan of modern painting. He also draws from early-twentieth-century designers associated with the Art Nouveau and Art Deco movements.

"The Art Nouveau and Art Deco movements were really a rebellion against industrialization—the mass-produced, factory-made furniture that was becoming popular at the end of the nineteenth century.

"Protesting against mechanization is not the reason I make furniture, of course. I drive a machine-made car every day. I use power tools. I'm not living in the woods; I'm not a Luddite. But I am making a complicated statement—if it can be called a statement—in my art: about how important it is to be connected to the objects in your environment and to interpret them. Objects don't come out of nowhere. Every time I create a new object, I'm responding to, and in some ways organizing, a history of ideas and forms."

—Jori Finkel

Fred Sway

JAMIE ROBERTSON

JAMIE ROBERTSON DESIGNS ▧ 43 BRADFORD STREET ▧ CONCORD, MA 01742 ▧ TEL 978-371-1106 ▧ FAX 978-371-1809
E-MAIL JAMBIA9@MSN.COM

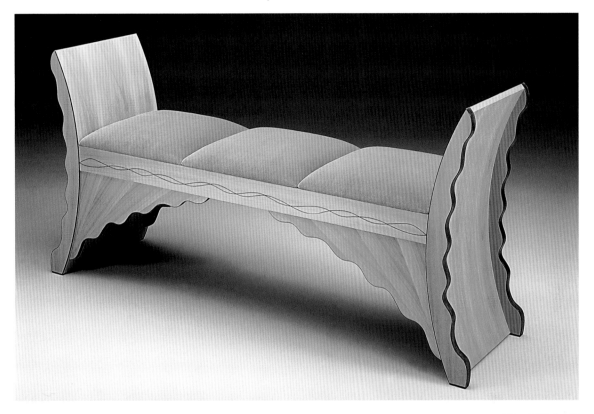

Top: *Water Bench*, 27"H × 58"W × 16"D. Photograph: Dean Powell. Bottom right: Media cabinet, 63"H × 51"W × 24"D. Photograph: Robertson & de Rham.
Bottom left: *Courtship in the Maze*, 64"H × 48"W × 3"D. Photograph: Dean Powell.

HOWARD HATCH

PO BOX 1467 ■ CONWAY, NH 03818 ■ TEL/FAX 603-447-8486 ■ E-MAIL HHATCH@NCIA.NET

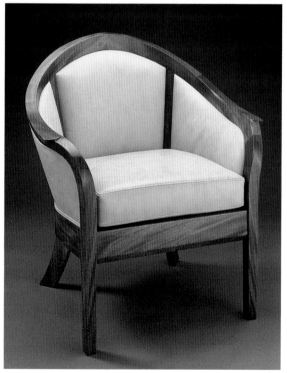

Top: Pool Table, 2002, private collection, mahogany and holly, 60" × 110" × 32"H. Photograph: Olof Ekbergh.
Bottom left: Barrel-back chair, 2000, private collection, mahogany and leather, 36" × 34" × 28" Photograph: Dean Powell.
Bottom right: Grid-back chair, 2001, private collection, cherry and fabric, 35" × 21" × 18". Photograph: Olof Ekbergh.

WILLIAM D. BOSWORTH

W.D. BOSWORTH WOODWORKING ■ 59 LUTHER WARREN DRIVE ■ ST. HELENA, SC 29920
TEL 843-838-9490 ■ FAX 843-838-1187 ■ E-MAIL WOODWORK@HARGRAY.COM ■ WWW.QUALITYWOODWORKING.COM

47

Top left: Plantation reclining bed (detail). Top right: Two-seated arbor, mahogany, 76"L x 30"W x 90"H.
Bottom: Plantation reclining bed (queen size), mahogany, 56"H x 66"W x 9'5"L. Photographs: N. White Photography.

JOHN SUTTMAN

PO BOX 27242 ■ ALBUQUERQUE, NM 87125 ■ TEL 505-453-8271 ■ FAX 505-352-2930
E-MAIL JPSUTTMAN@EARTHLINK.NET ■ WWW.JOHNSUTTMAN.COM

48

Left: *Vitrine Vitesse*, steel with patina, low-voltage lighting and beveled glass, 72" x 26" x 15".
Right: *Story Drawers*, steel with patina, mahogany, maple, beveled mirror and gilding, 75" x 23.5" x 20.5". Photographs: Robert Reck.

SCAVENGER FURNITURE ART, LLC

MARK ORR ■ 4237 LAKE FOREST DRIVE EAST ■ ANN ARBOR, MI 48108 ■ TEL 734-995-2140 ■ FAX 734-995-5065
E-MAIL SCAVENGERART@AOL.COM ■ WWW.SCAVENGERART.COM

49

Top left: Wall shelf, wood, found objects and antique shutters, 27" x 19" x 10". Right: Shutter bookcase, wood, found objects and antique shutters, 61" x 26" x 16".
Bottom left: 3-drawer jewelry box, wood, found objects and antique shutters, 16" x 12" x 10";
Small curio cabinet, wood, found objects and antique shutters, 27"x 8" x 8". Photographs: Steve Kuzma.

BORIS BALLY

BORIS BALLY, ATELIER ■ 789 ATWELLS AVENUE ■ PROVIDENCE, RI 02909 ■ TEL 401-277-8464 ■ FAX 401-277-0697
E-MAIL BAD4BORR@AOL.COM ■ WWW.BORISBALLY.COM

50

Top left and top right: *Transit Chairs*, 2002, recycled aluminum traffic signage, champagne cork feet and hardware, each: 48" × 16" × 21". Photographs: Jeff Johnson.
Bottom: *Urban Enamel Platters* (collection), 2001, recycled aluminum traffic signage and copper rivets, 3.5" × 25.5"Dia. or 1.5" × 16"Dia. Photograph: Dean Powell.

TALKING TO THE ARTIST
Boris Bally

A metalworker known for his industrial-strength designs, Boris Bally does not travel light. When he moved his home and studio from Pittsburgh, Pennsylvania, to Providence, Rhode Island, five years ago, he needed an 18-wheeler and a crane to haul a total of 36,000 pounds. "I tease my wife, who's a physician, all the time," he says. "She carries all of her work around with her in her head. I would rather drag my stuff around with me externally."

Bob Thayer

This "stuff" includes raw materials, machinery ranging from saws to a hydraulic press, and finished designs, mainly in the form of wearable sculpture and jewelry, flatware and furniture. Weighing in among his heaviest work—and also his most popular—is the *Transit Series:* bowls and chairs made out of aluminum street signs, which are bent into shape with great force.

Using street signs is more than a chance for the artist to flex some muscle, however. It's also an elegant form of recycling. "Our resources on the planet are finite, and the best test of an artist is how well we can use what we have at hand," says Bally.

His vision of art as recycling comes in part from his training as a goldsmith in Basel, Switzerland, shortly after high school. Given the value of gold, obsessive conserving is part of the trade. But Bally treats scraps of non-precious metal with the same kind of care. He frequents scrap yards and likes to walk his dogs straight to the neighbors' trash cans on garbage days. One of his biggest recycling projects has been collecting corks from around the world to use as feet for his *Transit Chairs.*

"I started using champagne corks as the feet of my *Transit Chairs.* The cork made the perfect foot because it's pliant and easy to replace. You just have to be willing to break open a champagne bottle in the name of art."

—Jori Finkel

PECK TILE, POTTERY & SCULPTURE

LEO PECK ■ 1065 LOS CARNEROS AVENUE ■ NAPA, CA 94559
TEL 707-226-3100 ■ FAX 707-255-6202 ■ E-MAIL LEO@PECKTILE.COM ■ WWW.PECKTILE.COM

52

Top: *Pablo the Dog in Java Juiced*, 18" × 33" × 33".
Bottom: *Four-Piece, Synchronized One-Man Band*, 17" × 42"Dia. Photographs: ©dkbphoto.com.

EILEEN JAGER

LIGHTHUNTER ■ ONE COTTAGE STREET ■ EASTHAMPTON, MA 01027 ■ TEL/FAX 413-527-2090
E-MAIL EJAGER@EARTHLINK.NET ■ WWW.EILEENJAGER.COM

53

Top left: *Fleur D'Ange*, 2001, glass mosaic table-fountain, 45" x 16". Top right: *Verde Bench*, 2002, glass mosaic bench, 70" x 18" x 19".
Bottom: *FloWing*, 2002, glass mosaic table-fountain, 54" x 32" x 16". Photographs: Tommy O. Elder.

FINDING ART
Consider the Source

Your search for a work of art can take many forms. It can be direct and methodical, as when you're looking for a vase or sculptural work to fit an oddly shaped alcove, or organic and adventurous, as when you're searching for a special something to mark a landmark anniversary. It can be the focus of a month of weekend outings to galleries, art fairs and artist studios, or an evening's pleasant browsing on the Internet. For more substantial purchases, especially those that involve complex installation, you may want to work with a professional art consultant or with the staff at GUILD's Custom Design Center.

Each of these methods of finding art has unique benefits. Let's begin with a look at buying art on the Internet, using the GUILD.com website as a practical model.

THE VIRTUAL SEARCH FOR ART

The Internet has revolutionized art buying, just as it has so many other aspects of our lives. A virtual gallery like GUILD.com offers distinctive benefits, especially if you're pressed for time, prefer to shop at night or want to see a very broad selection of quality artworks. By buying art gifts on the Internet, you also avoid having to ship fragile works yourself; at GUILD.com, for example, packing and shipping are handled by the artist— who knows better than anyone how to do it right.

Internet technology also allows you to search for art items meeting precise specifications. Looking through an extensive collection of online art is similar in many respects to visiting a large museum. Visitors to a museum can meander happily from room to room, browsing randomly, broadening their understanding of different art forms and perhaps kindling new enthusiasms. Alternately, they can use a map of the museum to select and visit the parts of the collection that interest them the most.

So it is with an online collection, except that instead of a map, the visitor uses searches to view the collection strategically. At GUILD.com, search criteria include medium, price range, color, theme and size, and they can be used singly or in any combination to fine-tune your search.

GUILD.com uses Internet technology to offer other services that are both useful and fun. E-postcards, for example, allow you to send images of favorite artworks to friends, with your own notes attached. GUILD's Wish List lets you keep a visual record of items you'd like to own someday, while the Gift Registry lets friends browse and shop from among items you've chosen. Another unique resource, the GUILD Custom Design Center, allows shoppers to have artworks customized to their specifications: a perfect way to celebrate a family milestone, fill an unusual space or make everyday objects artful.

When questions arise, or when you want to place custom orders, you can reach GUILD's knowledgeable staff toll-free. Call 1-877-344-8453 to place an order, or to find out more about individual artists or works of art.

55

Dana Lynne Anderson, *Mystic River*, painting. Photograph: Rosalie Wardell Photography.

GALLERIES

Purchasing from a gallery provides the benefit of consultation; you're tapping into the expertise of the gallery staff and the relative assurance that the work meets high aesthetic and professional standards. The artworks will have been selected by the gallery owner or manager, and will reflect their personal taste. If your own aesthetic is similar, a gallery can be an excellent resource.

Most galleries specialize in specific types of art and are committed to a stable of artists. Much like interior designers or art consultants, galleries act as professional curators; most select 20 to 50 artists to feature from among hundreds seeking representation.

To varying degrees, galleries act as agents for artists and help create a market for their work. It can be fun and interesting to attend gallery openings in your city or town. If the artwork you see appeals to you, introduce yourself to the gallery owner. Talk about your interest in purchasing art and about the kinds of work you're attracted to. Be sure to mention your budget—and don't feel intimidated if you don't want to spend a great deal of money. Galleries are always looking for new clients, and they'll be happy to spend time getting to know you.

BUYING DIRECTLY FROM THE ARTIST

Every artist whose work is shown in *The Artful Home* will welcome your phone call and your business. Look for their contact information at the top of their display page, as well as basic information about their products and processes in the Artist Information section at the back of the book.

Many artists keep at least a few completed works in the studio and can provide overnight turnaround for last-minute gifts and the like. This is most often true with artists who make small-scale works, but even artists who produce large-scale sculpture or furniture may keep a few available works on hand.

If you're not in a rush to buy, it can be fun to visit the artist's studio. When distance makes that impossible, ask to see photos of available works; photos can often be attached to e-mail if snail mail is too slow. And remember that *Artful Home* artists are available for custom-design projects; see Commissioning a Work of Art, beginning on page 16.

Studio Visits

When visiting an artist's studio, rules of common courtesy apply. Be sure to call ahead; the artist may have limited visiting hours, especially during crunch times. Once there, don't overstay your welcome. Enjoy your visit, but recognize that the artist will need to get back to work.

Some communities offer organized tours of artists' studios on a particular day or weekend each year. These are terrific opportunities to meet artists and learn about the processes they use.

Art Fairs

Depending upon the crowds and the weather (if the fair is outdoors), art fairs can be a lot of fun. They're also a great way to see the work of many artists at one time. Most art fairs are juried, so you can expect to see high-quality displays and meet artists who work at a professional level.

ART CONSULTANTS

Art consultants work with individuals and corporations, helping them select and place art. This is not a service you'll need for most purchases, but an art consultant can be a tremendous help with complex projects (see below). Although art consultants are familiar with the work of hundreds of artists—and may know many artists personally—they are engaged by, and represent the interests of, the art buyer. Normally, an art consultant is not affiliated with specific galleries or institutions.

Finding an art consultant in rural areas of the country can be a challenge. The Internet can be a great help, of course, and local architects and interior designers may recommend art consultants in your area or with whom they've had successful long-distance relationships. In any case, it's wise to talk with several art consultants to get a feel for the services they can offer and to gauge how comfortable you'll be working with them. Be sure to make reference calls as well, just as you would when hiring any service professional.

Art consultants are normally compensated through a percentage of the art-acquisition budget.

WHEN TO HIRE AN ART CONSULTANT

Art consultants can help with projects of any size and any medium. Their skills and experience are particularly helpful in these circumstances.

- When artwork is integral to the structure of the home, as with custom kitchen tile or a wrought iron balcony railing.

- When coordination is needed between the artist and other professionals, such as architects and engineers.

- When installation is complicated, as with heavy atrium sculpture or custom millwork.

- When art from several sources must coordinate, both functionally and aesthetically.

Opposite: Wendy Grossman, *pique assiette* bathroom installation (detail). Photographer: Steffany Rubin.

CHERYL HAZAN

ANANDAMALI, INC. ■ 35 NORTH MOORE STREET ■ NEW YORK, NY 10013
TEL 212-343-8964 ■ FAX 212-343-2544 ■ E-MAIL ANANDAMALI@AOL.COM

Top: *La Place Rouge* coffee table, 48" x 30" x 16"; *Rouge* dining table, 72" x 40" x 29".
Bottom: *Bamboo* console, solid walnut with glass mosaic, 48" x 16" x 29"; *Arbor* coffee table, solid walnut with glass mosaic, 36" x 36" x 16". Photographs: Vidura Barrios.

GRACE POMERLEAU FURNITURE STUDIO

GRACE POMERLEAU ■ 1519B SHELBURNE ROAD ■ SOUTH BURLINGTON, VT 05403
GRACE@GPFSTUDIO.COM ■ WWW.GPFSTUDIO.COM

Top left: Grecian bed (headboard detail). Top right: Grecian bed (corner flower detail).
Bottom: Grecian bed, 74"W x 91"L x 57"H. Photographs: ©2002 Carolyn Bates Photography.

BILL AND SANDY FIFIELD

THE STUDIO ■ PO BOX 366 ■ CONIFER, CO 80433
TEL 303-838-5072 ■ E-MAIL MACFIFIELD@ATT.NET ■ WWW.MACFIFIELD.COM

Twig Cabinet, 62.5" × 30" × 12".

KIMBERLY SOTELO

PO BOX 91 ■ WAVERLY, AL 36879 ■ TEL 334-887-6422
EMAIL KSOTELO@HOTMAIL.COM

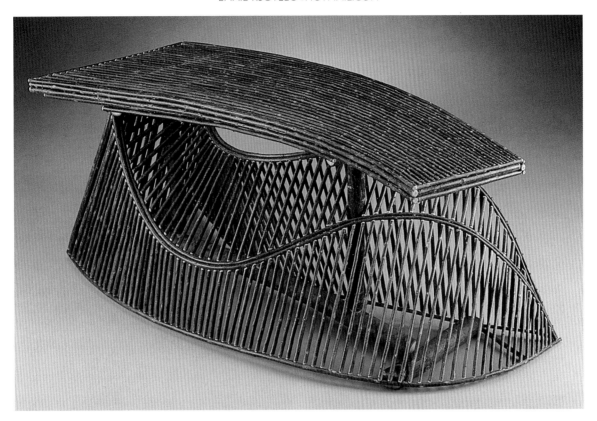

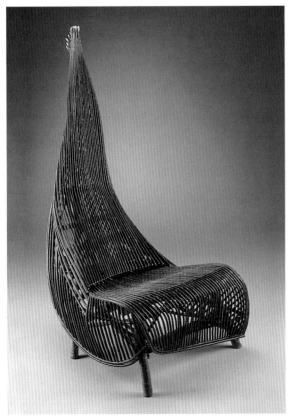

Top: *Mesa* coffee table, 20" × 52" × 24".
Bottom left: *Whoseville* chair, 42" × 32" × 36". Bottom right: *Whoseville* chair, back view.

MICHAEL DOERR

DOERR WOODWORKING ■ 4371 COUNTY HIGHWAY M ■ STURGEON BAY, WI 54235
TEL 920-743-5631 ■ E-MAIL MICHAEL@MICHAELDOERR.COM ■ WWW.MICHAELDOERR.COM

Top: Dinette set, curly maple. Photograph: Matt Orthober. Bottom right: Pedestal table, curly maple. Bottom left: *Bobbi's Chair*, curly maple.

MARK LEVIN

LEVIN STUDIO ▓ PO BOX 109 ▓ SAN JOSE, NM 87565-0109 ▓ TEL/FAX 505-421-3207
E-MAIL MARKLEVIN@MARKLEVIN.COM ▓ WWW.MARKLEVIN.COM

63

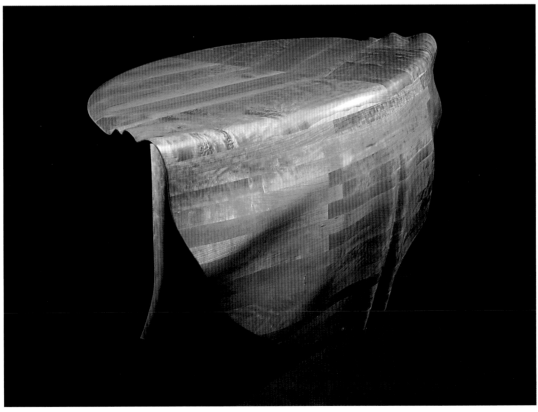

Top: *Jane Russell Leaf Hall Table*, mahogany with walnut detailing, 30" × 54" × 25".
Bottom: *Grace Kelly Leaf Desk*, cherry, 30" × 80" × 39". Photographs: Margot Geist.

DAVID EBNER

12 BELL STREET ■ BELLPORT, NY 11713 ■ TEL 631-286-4523 ■ FAX 631-286-2720 ■ E-MAIL DNEBNER@YAHOO.COM

Top left: Bench, cast bronze, 17" × 36" × 15.5". Top right: Corner table, cast bronze, 30.5" × 24" × 18". Center right: *Candle Holders II*, cast bronze, 15" × 3"Dia. and 10.5" × 2.5"Dia. Bottom right: *Renwick Stool*, cast bronze, 16.5" × 16" × 15". Bottom left: *Scallion Coat Rack*, cast bronze, 69"H × 15"W × 12.5"Dia. Photographs: Gil Amiaga.

ALAN ROSEN

ALAN ROSEN FURNITURE MAKERS LTD. ■ 3740 LEGOE BAY ROAD ■ LUMMI ISLAND, WA 98262
TEL 360-758-7452 ■ FAX 360-758-2498 ■ E-MAIL ALINDYROSEN@EARTHLINK.NET ■ WWW.ALANROSENFURNITURE.COM

65

Top: Padauk and ebony contemporary trestle table, 42" × 72" × 30". Photograph: Dana Kershner.
Bottom: Figured cherry and bubinga curved buffet, 22" × 60" × 36". Photograph: David Scherrer.

66

Top left: Cradle, ash and leather, 39" × 21" × 36". Top right: *Flower Stool*, 27" × 24" × 26", poplar and canary wood.
Bottom left: Youth chair/highchair, birdseye maple and zebrawood, 34" × 21" × 19". Bottom right: Hanging chair, ash, rosewood, leather and sheepskin, 70" × 35" × 35".

JAY WHYTE

INNOVATIVE DESIGNS IN WOOD ▓ 6620 DICK FORD LANE EAST ▓ KNOXVILLE, TN 37920
TEL 865-609-0313 ▓ E-MAIL JAYWHYTEDESIGNS@YAHOO.COM

Top left: Wavy-leg pedestal tablecloth, available in any wood combination, 32" x 14" x 22". Top right: Oriental-leg sofa tablecloth, available in any wood combination, 30" x 14" x 46".
Bottom left: *Lost in Space*, stack lamination vessel with lid, ebony, pink ivory and maple, 33" x 14" x 14".
Bottom right: *Cygnus X-1*, bleached maple burl with ebony trim and accents, stand: African bubinga, 14" x 7" x 7".

SCOTT BRAUN

SCOTT BRAUN FURNITURE, INC. ▪ 361 STAGG STREET SUITE #2L ▪ BROOKLYN, NY 11206 ▪ TEL 718-381-9200 ▪ FAX 718-381-0978
E-MAIL INFO@SCOTTBRAUNFURNITURE.COM ▪ WWW.SCOTTBRAUNFURNITURE.COM

68

Top: *b & w,* 2002, ebonized mahogany and calfskin, shown with *slung carlo,* 2001, black walnut and dyed leather.
Bottom: *mingreen* coffee and end tables, 2001, black walnut, 18"H x 21"W x 38"L and 23"H x 18"W x 28"L. Photographs: Eric McNatt.

GREGG LIPTON FURNITURE

GREGG LIPTON ■ I MILL RIDGE ROAD ■ CUMBERLAND, ME 04021 ■ TEL 207-829-5010 ■ FAX 207-829-3128
E-MAIL GREGG@LIPTONFURNITURE.COM ■ WWW.LIPTONFURNITURE.COM

69

Top left: *Gazelle Dining Table*, curly maple and cherry with ebony pinstripes; *Gazelle Dining Chair*, cherry, curly maple and leather.
Right: *Gramercy Stools*, maple, leather and stainless steel; cabinetry in European beech.
Bottom left: *Gazelle II Table*, cherry and "curly" stainless steel panels; *Tusk Side Chairs*, dyed maple, leather and bronze tacking.

HAMILTON S. DIXON

1001 EAST SECOND STREET ■ DAYTON, OH 45402 ■ TEL 937-228-3555
E-MAIL HBONE@SPRINGNET.CC ■ WWW.HAMILTONDIXON.COM

Top: *Jennifer's Bed*, forged steel, king-size. Bottom left: *Yanes's Table*, forged steel, 29.5" × 36"Dia.
Bottom right: *Katherine's Sculpture*, forged steel, 32" × 25" × 10". Photographs: Todd Champlin.

MOLLIE MASSIE

MYERS MASSIE STUDIO ■ PO BOX 30073 ■ 8602 GRANVILLE STREET ■ VANCOUVER, BC V6P 653 ■ CANADA
TEL 604-266-5009 ■ FAX 604-266-8431 ■ E-MAIL MOLLIE@MYERSMASSIESTUDIO.COM ■ WWW.MYERSMASSIESTUDIO.COM

Top left: *Rock Art* bar stools, Cor-ten steel, 40.5" × 17" × 19". Top right: *Leafing Out* fire screen, Cor-ten steel, 30" × 30".
Bottom left: *Life Story* fire screen, 30" × 30". Bottom right: *Globe* chandelier, 30" × 36". Photographs: Rob Melnychuk.

SUZANNE JANSE-VREELING

1935 LINCOLN STREET NE ■ MINNEAPOLIS, MN 55418-4741 ■ TEL 612-384-6719
E-MAIL SJANSEVREELING15@VISI.COM

72

Chair, metal, 18" x 42" x 18".

THE ROOMS OF YOUR HOME
The Entryway

The map of your home begins at its threshold. Doors and openings anchor the main thoroughfares and connect the outside world to your sanctuary within. Your entry also provides an excellent starting point for the practice of balancing function and comfort; it sets the stage for the style and mood that unfold as you move into your home. Lighting should be warm and easily adjustable, helping those who enter transition from outdoor light to the composed lighting within.

The artwork you place in the entryway creates the first impression guests receive of your home. Entryways are perfect spaces for small, framed artworks. The confined space encourages an intimate interaction between the viewer and the art. Small sculptures and objects can also be intriguing introductions to the story of your home.

Do your best to keep your entryway free of clutter and obstructions. Be sure that you have sufficient shelves, racks and hooks to store coats, hats, shoes and the like. Let the energy flow through this important channel, and don't hesitate to change the art on display, letting it evolve over time.

Above: Mollie Massie, *Spaceman* chair. Photograph: Rob Melnychuk. See pages 17 and 71.

SAM OSTROFF

SOUTH PAW STUDIOS ■ 69 PROSPECT STREET #41 ■ NORTHAMPTON, MA 01060
TEL 413-585-0240 ■ E-MAIL SAMYULE@AOL.COM ■ WWW.SAMOSTROFF.COM

Top left: Neo-gothic church pews, oak and steel, 7'L. Top right: Music stand/lectern #2, 2002, welded forged steel 62"H.
Bottom: *Rocketship* barstools, 2002, stainless steel and leather, 33"H.

FAUNA COLLECTION

1228 SOUTH HAYES ▨ FRESNO, CA 93706 ▨ TEL 559-268-1952 ▨ FAX 559-264-6524
E-MAIL FAUNA@CVIP.NET ▨ WWW.FAUNACOLLECTION.COM

Top left: *Rabbit Chair.* Top right: *Impala Chair.* Bottom left: *Eagle Chair.* Bottom right: *Dolphin Chair.*
All chairs: aluminum alloys with leather upholstery. Photographs: Bill Bachhuber.

JOHN LEWIS GLASS STUDIO

JOHN LEWIS ■ 10229 PEARMAIN STREET ■ OAKLAND, CA 94603 ■ TEL 510-635-4607 ■ FAX 510-569-5604
E-MAIL JLEWISGLS@AOL.COM ■ WWW.JOHNLEWISGLASS.COM

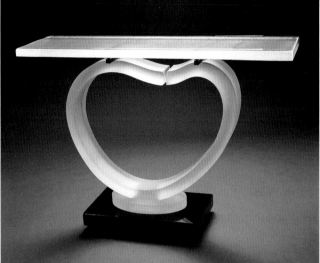

Top left: *Cone Table*, 2002, clear and black cast glass with copper patina, 29"H × 48"Dia.
Top right: *Impressed Coffee Table*, 2002, clear cast-glass elements, 18"H × 30"W × 18"D. Design by The Wiseman Group.
Bottom left: *Oval Coffee Table*, 2001, clear cast glass with copper patina, 20"H × 54"W × 37"D.
Bottom right: *Ribbon Console*, 2001, clear and black cast glass, 35"H × 50"W × 15"D. Photographs: Charles Frizzell.

LAVEZZO DESIGNS

JANEL AND ROBERT LAVEZZO ▨ 1218 24TH STREET ▨ OAKLAND, CA 94607 ▨ TEL 510-663-9157 ▨ FAX 510-663-9158
E-MAIL LAVEZZOMETAL@EARTHLINK.NET ▨ WWW.LAVEZZODESIGNS.COM

Top: *A Bench for Castillo,* darkened steel, 21" × 51" × 16", limited edition.
Bottom: *River Rock* foyer table, hand-brushed steel and slate with inset steel ellipsoids, 36" × 36" × 29.5"H, limited edition.

HARRIETT BELAG

HARRIETT BELAG STUDIO ▦ 3333 HENRY HUDSON PARKWAY 2S ▦ RIVERDALE, NY 10463
TEL 718-601-0893 ▦ FAX 718-601-7552 ▦ E-MAIL HBELAGLANGE@MSN.COM

Top left: *Fruitful*, oil-painted stoneware lamp, 55" × 26" × 17". Top right: *Holding It Together*, oil-painted stoneware chair, 45" × 18" × 22".
Bottom left: *Balancing Act*, oil-painted stoneware chair, 51" × 21" × 18". Bottom right: *Jewels*, oil-painted stoneware chair, 46" × 21" × 18".

HARRIETT BELAG

HARRIETT BELAG STUDIO ▨ 3333 HENRY HUDSON PARKWAY 2S ▨ RIVERDALE, NY 10463
TEL 718-601-0893 ▨ FAX 718-601-7552 ▨ E-MAIL HBELAGLANGE@MSN.COM

Top left: *Le Cirque*, oil-painted stoneware and wood chair, 68" x 18" x 19". Top right: *Isn't It Romantic*, oil-painted stoneware chair, 51" x 20" x 21".
Bottom: *Conversation*, oil-painted stoneware and wood bench, 49" x 62" x 21".

BETH M. LIPPERT

MONKEY BUSINESS LLC ■ 1650 RIVER MILL ROAD ■ OSHKOSH, WI 54901 ■ TEL 920-203-9101
E-MAIL BETH@MONKEYBUSINESSLLC.COM ■ WWW.MONKEYBUSINESSLLC.COM

Top: Collection of artwork. Bottom left: *Ride 'em Cowboy*, children's rocking horse, 26" × 9" × 18.5".
Bottom right: *"D" is for Dog*, children's table and chair set, 36" × 23" × 33". Photographs: Dylan Stolley.

THE ROOMS OF YOUR HOME
Kids' Rooms

If you have young children, your home will often feel overrun with their playthings. Between Barbie and Barney and all the other kid gear, there may be moments when your home feels more like a sanitarium than a sanctuary.

Children change quickly as they grow up, and their surroundings need to reflect this fact. Keep this in mind when decorating and furnishing their rooms. Children's rooms should be simple and cozy—and flexible enough to allow changes as the kids grow and mature. Involve them in the design of their rooms and share the decision-making process. Include them when choosing colors and engage them in the painting and furnishing experience.

Use your kids' rooms to stimulate creativity and to introduce them to art. If you can, consider commissioning an artist to do a custom mural on the walls or ceilings of your child's room. If your budget won't stretch that far, consider artist-made, child-size furniture or bright, cheerful prints framed with unbreakable plexiglass. The artworks we see when we're children are vividly fixed in our memories, so these are important choices.

Golds, pinks and greens harmonize in the playful yet functional furniture of this inviting children's space.
Interior design by Mary Drysdale. Photograph: Andrew Lautman.

ZEN STONE FURNISHINGS

CLEO AND SOLOMON HILL ▧ 307 JOHNSON STREET ▧ SANTA FE, NM 87501 ▧ TEL/FAX 505-955-0906 / 888-334-9168 (TOLL FREE)
EMAIL INFO@ZENSTONELIGHTING.COM ▧ WWW.ZENSTONELIGHTING.COM

Zen Stone Furnishings, 2002: *Zen Buffet Table,* mixed media, 35"H x 67"L x 20"W;
Rock Tower Lamp with New Green, hand-made paper shade, mixed media, 35"H. Red wall sconce. Photograph: Eric Swanson/The Santa Fe Catalogue.

LIGHTING

ROCK COTTAGE GLASSWORKS, INC.

DIERK VAN KEPPEL ■ 6801 FARLEY AVENUE ■ MERRIAM, KS 66203 ■ TEL 913-262-1763 ■ FAX 913-262-0430
E-MAIL RCGLASS@GRAPEVINE.NET ■ WWW.VANKEPPELARTGLASS.COM

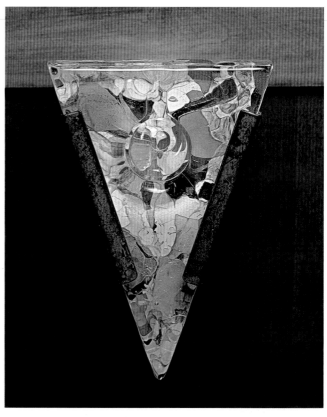

Top left: *Clam Shell* pendants, 2001, blown glass, each: 10" × 10". Top right: *Pierpont Booth* sconce, 2001, cast glass, 12" × 8".
Bottom right: Pendant lights, 2001, blown glass, 7" × 6". Bottom left: Gilman restoration, 2001, blown glass, each: 7" × 6.5". Photographs: Tim Pott.

PAM MORRIS DESIGNS EXCITING LIGHTING

PAM MORRIS ■ 14 EAST SIR FRANCIS DRAKE BOULEVARD STUDIO D ■ LARKSPUR, CA 94939
TEL 415-925-0840 ■ FAX 415-925-1305 ■ E-MAIL LIGHTING@SONIC.NET

85

Wave Pendant, kiln-formed glass, 32" x 32".

BARBARA FLETCHER

PAPER DIMENSIONS ▩ 23 JENNINGS ROAD ▩ BILLERICA, MA 01862 ▩ TEL 617-268-8644 ▩ FAX 978-670-5290
E-MAIL BARBARA@PAPERDIMENSIONS.COM ▩ WWW.PAPERDIMENSIONS.COM

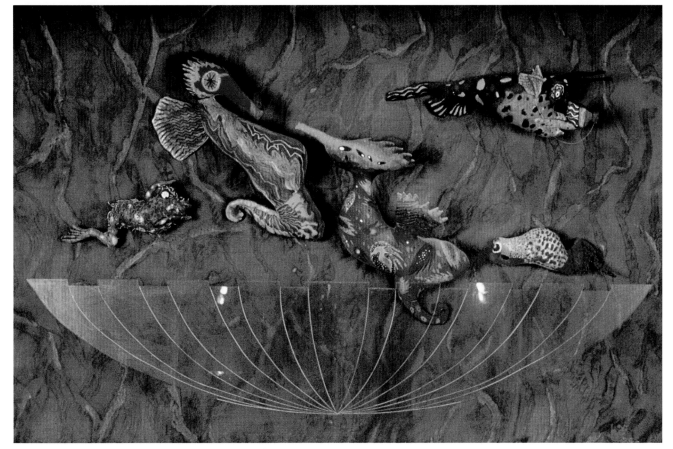

Top left: Fish Lamps, 2000, paper pulp and wire, 21" x 12" x 13" and 23" x 18" x 12".
Top right: Frog and Heron Lamps, 2002, paper pulp and wire, heron: 24" x 19" x 5", frog: 14" x 11" x 10". Photographs: Gordon Bernstein.
Bottom: Seahorses, fiber with Plexiglas half-shell, wall-mounted, 2' x 4' x 2".

DIANA HARRISON

ILLUMINART ■ 25 LITTLE CREEK LANE ■ MIDDLETOWN, RI 02842 ■ TEL 401-847-4924 ■ FAX 401-846-6695
ILL0748@AOL.COM ■ WWW.CORRIECROFT.COM

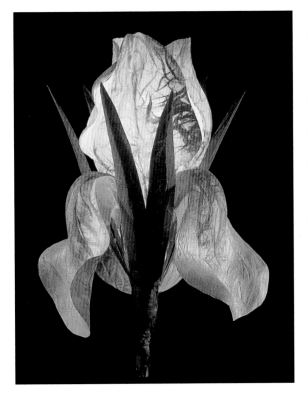

Top left: Iris lamp. Photograph: Marc Harrison. Top right: Bedroom with *Large Angels Trumpet*, 43"H. Photograph: John Harkey. Bottom: *White* chandelier. Photograph: John Harkey.

THE ROOMS OF YOUR HOME
The Kitchen

The kitchen is the heart of the home—and its central nervous system as well. In many modern homes, the family also spends much of its "together time" in the kitchen, and cooking and conversation are the main events. Most families prefer large eat-in kitchens, with quiet dining rooms reserved for holidays and special occasions.

Our kitchens generate the food we eat and represent the bounty of the earth. Food has always been an inspirational subject for painters; they celebrate fruits, grains and vegetables, as well as the spirit of the vine. These kinds of images are very much at home in a kitchen. Since wall space is often limited, small framed pieces are usually best.

The kitchen is also a wonderful place to display objects and tools. Wood, glass and ceramic are the materials of choice for the kitchen: handcrafted wooden bowls, blown glass toasting goblets and glazed stoneware tiles and storage containers complement and enhance the kitchen environment. Handmade tabletop items can be beautifully displayed on open shelves alongside your herbs, dressings and jams. All of these artworks can soothe and calm what is often a hectic pace in these increasingly high-tech spaces.

Above: Gregg Lipton Furniture, *Gramercy Stools.* See page 69.

WILLIAM AND RENEE MORRIS

THE WILLIAM MORRIS STUDIO ■ 1716 ELLIE COURT ■ BENICIA, CA 94510 ■ TEL/FAX 707-745-3907
E-MAIL WILLIAM@WILLIAMMORRISSTUDIO.COM ■ WWW.WILLIAMMORRISSTUDIO.COM

89

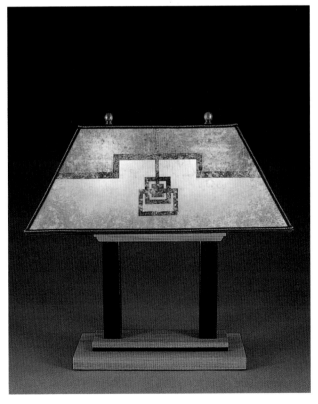

Top: *Oliver*, hand-blown art glass, cherry, mica shade with Japanese maple leaves, 15" × 19.5"Dia., glass by Joseph Morell. Photograph: Linda Svendsen.
Bottom left: *Silent Times*, Honduras mahogany and amber mica with Japanese maple leaves, 20.5" × 24"H.
Bottom right: *Library Interlocking Square*, Honduras mahogany and alkyd mica with handcut motif, 20" × 18.5"H. Photograph: Carl Nelson.

RED FERN GLASS

ED PENNEBAKER ■ 428 COUNTY ROAD 9351 ■ GREEN FOREST, AR 72638 ■ TEL 877-553-2592 ■ FAX 775-254-6321
E-MAIL ED@REDFERNGLASS.COM ■ WWW.REDFERNGLASS.COM

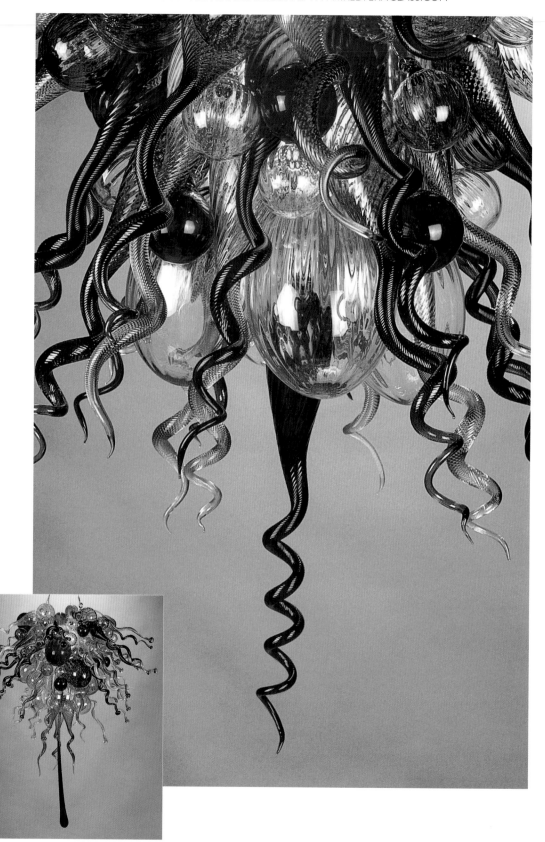

Inset: Multicolor chandelier #119, 2001, glass, 37"H x 37"Dia.
Red/amber/smoke chandelier #118, 2001, glass, 26"H x 35"Dia. Photographs: Michael Crow, Zendeux Visual Captivation.

ARCHITECTURAL DETAILS

GLENN F. GILMORE

GILMORE METALSMITHING STUDIO ■ PO BOX 961 ■ HAMILTON, MT 59840 ■ TEL/FAX 406-961-1861
E-MAIL GLENN@GILMOREMETAL.COM ■ WWW.GILMOREMETAL.COM

Top: Fireplace doors and hearth tools, private residence, Vail, Colorado, forged mild steel, copper and Pyroceram glass, 46" x 48". Photograph: McNabb Studio.
Bottom: Fireplace doors and hearth tools, private residence, coastal South Carolina, forged mild steel and stainless steel, 31" x 39". Photograph: Ron Blunt.

GLENN F. GILMORE

GILMORE METALSMITHING STUDIO ■ PO BOX 961 ■ HAMILTON, MT 59840 ■ TEL/FAX 406-961-1861
E-MAIL GLENN@GILMOREMETAL.COM ■ WWW.GILMOREMETAL.COM

Top left: Fireplace doors, private residence, forged mild steel, stainless steel and Pyroceram glass, 42" x 48". Top right: *Ship's Wheel* fireplace doors, anchor andirons and hearth tools, private residence, forged mild steel, bronze, brass and stainless steel, 32" x 31". Bottom right: Fireplace screen and hearth tools, private residence, forged navel bronze and stainless steel, 32" x 30". Bottom left: Fireplace doors and hearth tools, steel and repousse copper, 36" x 40". Photographs: McNabb Studio.

STEVE HASSLOCK

HASSLOCK STUDIOS ■ 334 NORTH VERMONT ■ COVINGTON, LA 70433
TEL 985-893-6648 ■ FAX 985-893-0083 ■ E-MAIL TIKA@AIRMAIL.NET ■ WWW.HASSLOCKSTUDIOS.COM

94

Top: Fireplace, clay work. Bottom: Fireplace (detail). Photographs: Philip Gould.

EARTH FIRE DESIGNS

FREDERICK MICHAEL KING ■ 740 METCALF SUITE #29 ■ ESCONDIDO, CA 92025 ■ TEL 760-747-3347 ■ FAX 760-871-3348
E-MAIL MICHAEL@EARTHFIREDESIGNS.COM ■ WWW.EARTHFIREDESIGNS.COM

Moroccan fireplace, clay with copper inlay, 68" x 65".

LEARNING TO SEE

To develop a personal aesthetic—the value system that defines our sense of beauty, grace and comfort—we must learn to look with a critical eye at everything that surrounds us. When we study the architecture of our living environment, the array of furnishings we select and the art we acquire, we should be able to recognize how these pieces work together to balance the many elements of design: color, texture, form and proportion. Developing this ability is what we call "learning to see."

An important aspect of creating a personal aesthetic involves cultivating a point of view with regard to material possessions, a point of view based on the goals of your space. Learning to see requires that you look at many objects and absorb what each one has to offer without losing sight of your own circumstances and needs. You can accomplish this by developing a dialogue with an object. No, we don't mean speaking out loud to it, but rather becoming curious about it. Where is it from? How old is it? Was it crafted by hand or by machine? What unusual techniques were used to produce it? Did its creator sign it? Finding the answers to these questions will enrich your understanding and deepen your appreciation of the object you're looking at. This process increases your knowledge, strengthens your personal aesthetic, and prepares your eye to seek beauty in all that it sees.

Unique floor and table-top sculptures are placed to give this otherwise symmetrical room a delightful sense of surprise. Interior design by Mary Drysdale. Photograph: Andrew Lautman.

The art you acquire and objects that you collect each have a story. When brought together in your home, they tell a unique story about you. It's your goal to become a good storyteller.

When you introduce art into your home, you're adding a layer onto a foundation established through the furnishings, lighting and accessories that you've inherited or purchased over time. These possessions were doubtless acquired as much for their function as for taste and style. Creating an artful home is about selecting and placing art that complements your foundation of core furnishings while celebrating beauty and spirit and reflecting something intimate about you and your family.

Looking at art feels very different from looking at other kinds of furnishings. An artist's work can take you by surprise. It can inspire pleasure, confusion or an immediate sense of affinity. You may like what you're looking at, or you may not. Either way, your eye is stimulated, and the piece calls to you for response and reaction.

The wonderful thing about art is that it need not be constrained by anything more than your personal aesthetic: "Wow! I like that! Now, where in my home can I place that for all my friends and family to see?" Suddenly you're engaged. You're thinking about how to share the story. That's the fun and the beauty of learning to see.

LOUIS DeMARTINO

LOUIS DeMARTINO ARCHITECTURAL SCULPTOR ■ BOX 391370 ■ ANZA, CA 92539 ■ TEL 909-763-1315 ■ FAX 909-763-2360
E-MAIL LOUIS@LOUISDEMARTINO.COM ■ WWW.LOUISDEMARTINO.COM

98

Left: Bronze fountain, private residence, Coronado Island, CA, 16'H. Right: Sculpted bronze doors and window, door: 6'x 8', window: 8'.

STEVE FONTANINI

STEVE FONTANINI ARCHITECTURAL & ORNAMENTAL BLACKSMITHING ▧ PO BOX 2298 ▧ 11400 SOUTH HOBACK JUNCTION ROAD
JACKSON, WY 83001 ▧ TEL 307-733-7668 ▧ FAX 307-734-8816 ▧ E-MAIL SFONTANI@WYOMING.COM

Forged bronze railing of winter aspen trees and birds, Roney residence, Teton County, WY. Photograph: Florence McCall.

JORDAN

JORDAN METAL WORKS ▩ 1434 COUNTY ROAD 106 ▩ ETNA, WY 83118 ▩ TEL 307-883-8201 ▩ FAX 307-883-8200
E-MAIL JORDANMETALWORKS@SILVERSTAR.COM

100

Top: *Elk Drive Gates,* 2002, stainless steel and copper repoussé elk, design by Don Fredrickson Design Source Inc. Photograph: Laura Sproull.
Bottom: Copper hood, 2002, hand-worked copper hood with wrought iron trim, design by Don Fredrickson Design Source Inc.

TRIO DESIGN GLASSWARE

RENATO FOTI ■ 253 QUEEN STREET SOUTH ■ KITCHENER, ON N2G 1W4 ■ CANADA
TEL 519-749-2814 ■ FAX 519-749-6319 ■ E-MAIL RENATOFOTI@ROGERS.COM ■ WWW.TRIODESIGNGLASSWARE.COM

Top left: *Geo Square*-style fused and thermal-sealed door panels, 2001, 72" × 85". Top right: *Geo Square*-style fused glass ceiling lamp, 2001, 24"Dia.
Bottom: *Geo Square*-style fused glass sink, 2001, 47" × 21". Photographs: JPB Photography.

DALE JENSSEN

PO BOX 129 ■ TERLINGUA, TX 79852 ■ TEL/FAX 432-371-2312
E-MAIL JENSSENGALLERY@HOTMAIL.COM ■ WWW.DALEJENSSEN.COM

102

Bathroom interior, 2002, private commission, wood, paint, steel, copper, cement, ceramic tile, plastic and miscellaneous recycled elements. Photograph: Blair Pittman.

JUDY MINER

JUDY MINER CUSTOM PORCELAIN ■ 2510 BELKNAP BEACH ■ PROSPECT, KY 40059
TEL 502-228-4812 ■ FAX 502-228-5034

Top: Basin, 2002, private residence, handmade porcelain, 18" × 5.5".
Bottom: Cabinet pulls, handmade, high fired porcelain, each approximately: 1.5"Dia. × 1.5"H. Photographs: Craig Guyon.

BJ KATZ

MELTDOWN GLASS ART AND DESIGN ▨ PO BOX 3850 ▨ CHANDLER, AZ 85244-3850 ▨ TEL 480-633-3366 ▨ FAX 480-633-3344
E-MAIL BJKATZ@MELTDOWNGLASS.COM ▨ WWW.MELTDOWNGLASS.COM

 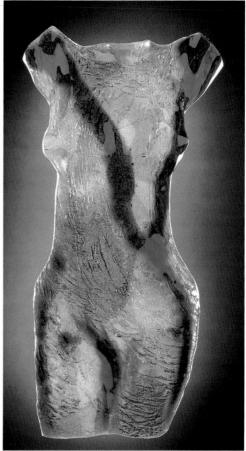

Top left: *Hera*, female torso from *Winged Victory*, 2000, cast and sand-carved glass, 30" × 20" × 6", limited series of 500. Photograph: Daniel Braha.

Top right: *Contemplation*, female torso from *Winged Victory*, 2000, cast and sand-carved glass.

Bottom: *Sea Life Scene*, 1999, private collection, Phoenix, AZ, cast glass, 36" × 78". Photograph: Daniel Braha.

Opposite page: *Joy of Creativity*, 1999, Sheraton Hotel, Phoenix, AZ, cast glass, 120" × 60". Photograph: Robin Stancliff.

FRANK J. SANTOVIZ, JR.

TAHOE DESIGN GROUP ■ 461 ZEHNDER DRIVE ■ FRANKENMUTH, MI 48734 ■ TEL 888-878-4378 ■ FAX 989-652-0090
E-MAIL FSANTOVIZ@TAHOEDESIGNGROUP.COM ■ WWW.TAHOEDESIGNGROUP.COM

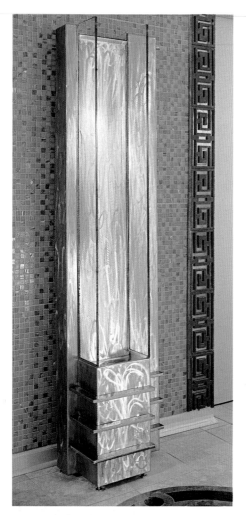

Top left: *Serenity*, flowing water sculpture, stainless steel, 72" × 18" × 11". Top right: *Arch Vanity*, aluminum, stainless steel, stained glass and Corian®, 34" × 60" × 24".
Bottom right: Dupont Corian® island top, stone countertop and backsplash. Bottom left: Dupont Corian® countertop with marble and granite inlays (detail). Photographs: Lloyd C. Wright.

DOORS, WINDOWS & SCREENS

LARRY ZGODA

LARRY ZGODA STUDIO ■ 2117 WEST IRVING PARK ROAD ■ CHICAGO, IL 60618 ■ TEL 773-463-3970
FAX 773-463-3978 ■ E-MAIL LZ@LARRYZGODASTUDIO.COM ■ WWW.LARRYZGODASTUDIO.COM

Untitled entry, 2001, private residence, Chicago, IL. Photograph: Richard Bruck.

MAYA RADOCZY

CONTEMPORARY ART GLASS ■ PO BOX 31422 ■ SEATTLE, WA 98103
TEL 206-527-5022 ■ FAX 206-524-9226 ■ E-MAIL MAYA@SERV.NET ■ WWW.MAYAGLASS.COM

Perry residence, 2001, Medina, WA, bas-relief cast glass doors. Photograph: Dick Springgate.

MASAOKA GLASS DESIGN

ALAN MASAOKA ▨ 13766 CENTER STREET SUITE G-2 ▨ CARMEL VALLEY, CA 93924 ▨ TEL 831-659-4953 ▨ FAX 831-659-3156
E-MAIL MASAOKA@MBAY.NET ▨ WWW.ALANMASAOKA.COM

Bath glass, 1998, Timkins residence, lead with handblown glass and bevels. Photograph: Philip Harvey.

MASAOKA GLASS DESIGN

ALAN MASAOKA ■ 13766 CENTER STREET SUITE G-2 ■ CARMEL VALLEY, CA 93924 ■ TEL 831-659-4953 ■ FAX 831-659-3156
E-MAIL MASAOKA@MBAY.NET ■ WWW.ALANMASAOKA.COM

111

Entry glass, 2002, Quail Meadows home, lead with handmade glass and bevels. Photograph: Philip Harvey.

TUSKA INC.

SETH TUSKA ▨ 147 OLD PARK AVENUE ▨ LEXINGTON, KY 40502
TEL 859-255-1379 ▨ FAX 859-253-3199 ▨ WWW.TUSKASTUDIO.COM

112

Illuminate bath screen, wood and Oguru paper, two panels, each: 62" x 20". Photograph: Lee Thomas.

SANDRA CHRISTINE Q. BERGÉR

QUINTAL STUDIO ■ 100 EL CAMINO REAL SUITE #202 ■ BURLINGAME, CA 94010
TEL 650-348-0310 ■ FAX 650-348-8733 ■ WWW.QUINTALSTUDIO.COM

Top: *Moonset*, residential entrance, art glass and prisms in walnut doors, 52"Dia.
Bottom: *All Seasons*, multicolored screen, 7' x 8' x 3". Photograph: William A. Porter, San Francisco, CA.

THE ROOMS OF YOUR HOME
The Living Room

The living room, where you gather with family and friends, is the most theatrical space in your home. Think of it as your gallery, your primary space for displaying and enjoying original works of art.

Abandon reality for a moment and envision your living room as a clean, empty white space. Now imagine placing favorite framed artworks and objects in their best possible locations, along with handmade, artist-designed furniture and furnishings chosen to complement the artworks. Of course, in reality you're unlikely to buy new furniture and furnishings to enhance each new piece of art you bring into your home. Still, it can be useful to think about how artwork would function in your ideal setting; we recommend you practice this pleasant exercise when considering new art purchases for this most important family space.

One common focal point in many living rooms is the fireplace, and the mantel and wall above it are perfect locations for framed artworks, small sculptures, family photos

Above: Hye Sun Baik, *Meditative Journey* (left) and *Inner Focus* (right), mixed-media wall hangings. Photograph: Glenda Kapsalis.

and handcrafted candleholders or other decorative objects. The artworks you place in this area comprise a still life, a vignette celebrating fine craftsmanship. By refreshing this setting periodically—and expanding it to the entire area surrounding the fireplace—you have the opportunity to seek out new works made by artists: forged-iron tools, hand-woven baskets, a rocker, original area rugs. The warmth of this setting is created as much by the artworks as by the fire.

In many homes, the living room is both the most public part of the home and a hub of family activity. Day-to-day, it's the family's gathering place; on special occasions, it's the setting for entertaining guests. It's almost always the largest room in the home and is usually positioned near the entryway. All of these qualities make the living room an ideal location for displaying large works of art, works that make the room inviting, yet dramatic and expressive. Its size also makes it flexible space, allowing for a variety of arrangements and focal points.

TIPS FOR AN ARTFUL HOME
Light Glimmers Through Glass

Our eye for beauty is cultivated by two primary sensory components of vision: light and color. In this setting, architectural colored glass is inset within perfectly proportioned door panels. The glass gently filters the natural light while simultaneously welcoming it into the room. Take advantage of colored art glass in all forms to keep your home feeling illuminated and vibrant.

Dick Weiss, glass doors. Rondels blown by Ben Moore and Sonja Blomdahl. Photograph: Magie Soladay. See pages 118-119.

SLEDD/WINGER GLASSWORKS

NANCY SLEDD ■ MARY LU WINGER ■ 1912 EAST MAIN STREET ■ RICHMOND, VA 23223
TEL 804-644-2837 ■ FAX 804-644-6821 ■ E-MAIL SLEDDWINGER@AOL.COM

Antoinette room divider, 1996, stained, beveled and etched glass, crystals and jewels, 70" x 66". Photograph: Tony Sylvestro.

DICK WEISS

DICK WEISS STUDIOS ▨ 811 NORTH 36TH STREET ▨ SEATTLE, WA 98103 ▨ TEL 206-632-8873

118

Zag-Zig, 2000, leaded glass screen, 4 panels, each: 90" x 20" x 1.75", rondels blown by Katherine Gray, Kait Rhoads, Sonja Blomdahl and Dante Marioni. Photograph: Russell Johnson.

Zirkus, 1998, leaded glass screen, 3 panels, each: 78" × 26" × 1.5", rondels blown by Sonja Blomdahl. Photograph: Russell Johnson.

JENNIFER JACOBY

8614 108 A STREET ■ EDMONTON, ALBERTA T6E 4M8 ■ CANADA
TEL 403-901-7043/780-432-5187 ■ E-MAIL JENNJACOB@YAHOO.COM

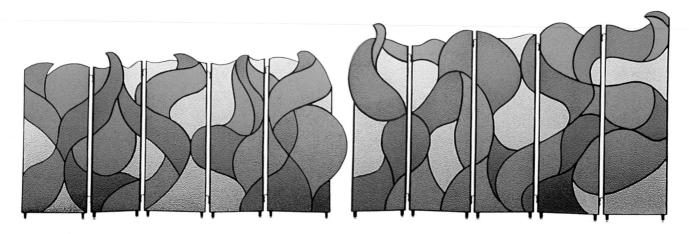

120

Top: Room divider/screen (two part), 2002, private residence, France, powder-coated steel and flat glass, 240" × 70".
Bottom: Change screen/room divider (two part), 2001, powder-coated steel, flat glass and fired paint, 138" × 68". Photographs: Darren Cockx, Image Works.

FLOOR COVERINGS

CALLAHAN McDONOUGH

RUBY SLIPPERS STUDIO ■ 512 HAROLD AVENUE ■ ATLANTA, GA 30307 ■ TEL 404-373-7370
E-MAIL RUBYSLIPPERSSTUDIO@MINDSPRING.COM ■ WWW.RUBYSLIPPERSSTUDIO.COM

122

Circle of Light, hemmed canvas and acrylic floorcloth, 6' × 8'.

TIPS FOR AN ARTFUL HOME
Magic Carpets and Polished Wood

Polished wood floors present artists with intriguing opportunities to show off original carpet designs. This unusual piece is a good example. Its size gives it a commanding presence, and the rich colors are enhanced by repeated patterns and narrative content. Notice how nicely the red velvet banister cover ties in with the colors of the rug itself.

Train yourself to think of your floors as surfaces available for distinctive works of art. Floor-level artworks create boundaries within a room, while adding color and texture to the surroundings.

Lynn Basa, *Wild Freedom*, wool rug. Photograph: Russell Johnson.

BENNETT BEAN STUDIO

357 ROUTE 661 ◼ BLAIRSTOWN, NJ 07825 ◼ TEL 908-852-8953
E-MAIL BENNETTBEAN@BENNETTBEAN.COM ◼ WWW.BENNETTBEAN.COM

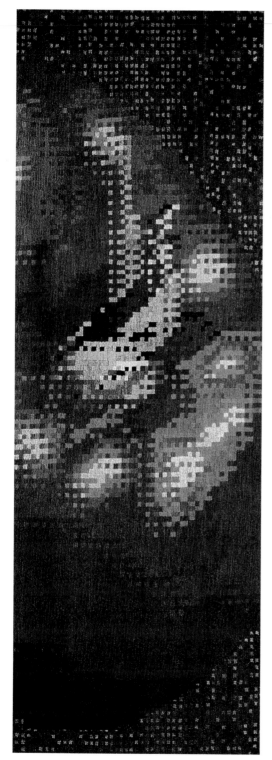

124

Left: *Hot Tomato*, rug from the *Botanical* series. Top right: *Red Zed*, rug. Bottom right: *12 Lemons*, rug from the *Botanical* series.

TABLETOP

MARGE MARGULIES

MARGE MARGULIES POTTERY ▨ 6801 SPRAGUE STREET ▨ PHILADELPHIA, PA 19119 ▨ TEL 215-844-9603
E-MAIL MARGE@MARGEMARGULIESPOTTERY.COM ▨ WWW.MARGEMARGULIESPOTTERY.COM

126

Top: 10-piece *Cabbage Rose* with platter, 18"W. Bottom: *Mille Feuille* plate composition, 12"W. Photographs: Elena Bouvier.

Quadrille dinnerware, assorted plates and soup bowl, porcelain with 22K gold details. Photograph: Lisa Charles Watson.

Reefscape series, 2002, turquoise, lemon and ruby glass lip salad bowl. Photograph: Marty Kelly.
Bottom: *Lemonfrost* martinis, pitcher and emerald lamp, 2002. Photograph: Paul Schraub.

129

Handcrafted glass tableware, 2002. Photograph: Paul Schraub.

MARKUSEN METAL STUDIOS LTD.

THOMAS MARKUSEN ■ 17218 ROOSEVELT HIGHWAY ■ KENDALL, NY 14476-9762 ■ TEL 585-659-8001 ■ FAX 585-659-8888
E-MAIL MARKUSENMETAL@ATT.NET ■ WWW.MARKUSENMETAL.COM

Top left: *340P*, 2002, copper oxide, brass and laminated metal tondo, 24" x 30". Top right: *748D* (dish candleholders), *748V* (vase), 2000, plasma-cut copper oxide and brass, candleholders: 6"D x 12"H, vase: 4" x 7" x 15"H. Bottom left: *126D*, 2001, copper oxide and brass dish candleholders, 4" x 18", 24" and 30"H with 9"Dia. dish. Bottom right: *660B*, 2000, copper oxide bowl with black oxide wire on black oxide bronze-cast base, 12"D x 12"H. Photographs: Bob Barrett.

THE ROOMS OF YOUR HOME
The Dining Room

The dining room is where family and friends gather around the table to share good meals, stimulating conversation and memorable stories. Just as you strive to please guests with your hospitality, menu selection, background music and lighting, so should you choose artworks that encourage a convivial mood.

The dining room is an ideal setting for art that elicits a meaningful story. Guests will notice the work displayed in the room and ask you about it. Sharing a unique story about the artist or about how you acquired the work reveals something about your interests and gives your friends a more complete sense of who you are.

Like the kitchen, the dining room is a natural setting for art that relates to food and eating. Since most dining rooms are adjacent to the kitchen, be sure to consider the relationship between the two rooms when contemplating the placement of art.

Above: Pam Morris Designs Exciting Lighting, *Wave Pendant*, glass lighting fixture. See page 85.

JANET TORELLI

JANET TORELLI, HANDCRAFTED SILVER ■ 451 WEST OAKDALE AVENUE ■ CHICAGO, IL 60657
TEL 773-388-2388 ■ FAX 773-388-9336 ■ E-MAIL JANET@MARTINIPIC.COM ■ WWW.MARTINIPIC.COM

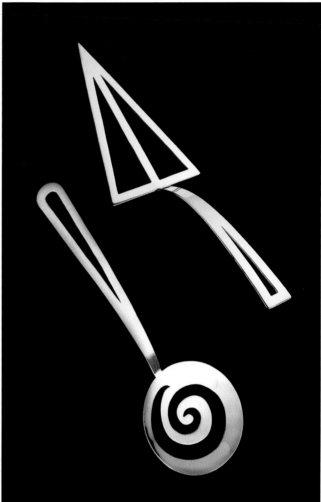

Top left: *Ginkgo* serving tong, 1998, sterling silver, 2" x 7.5", shown with *Spear* serving tong, 1999, sterling silver, 2" x 7.5".
Top right: *Swirl* tomato spoon, 2002, sterling silver, shown with *Arrow* cake server, 2001, sterling silver.
Bottom: *Petals and Leaves* martini/hors d'oeuvres picks, 2001 and 1996, sterling silver, 4.75". Photographs: Curtis Kulp.

LISA SLOVIS

LISA SLOVIS METALSMITHING ▨ 1730 PACIFIC BEACH DRIVE #3 ▨ SAN DIEGO, CA 92109 ▨ TEL 858-490-1336
E-MAIL LISA@LISASLOVIS.COM ▨ WWW.LISASLOVIS.COM

133

Top: Teapots, Vases and Salt and Pepper shakers, pewter. Bottom: *Mountain Menorah*, pewter and bronze, 2.5"–4".

TIPS FOR AN ARTFUL HOME
Industry Meets Art

The art you live with enriches your home all the more when it tells something about who you are. Think about this quality as you consider what kinds of artwork to acquire and where to display it. The bold, colorful dining table and chairs in this setting, for example, complement the industrial aesthetic of the architecture while also expressing a great sense of fun and inventiveness. At the same time, they provide both a functional stage for dining and entertaining and an important focal point for the large open space. The tapestry in the background is a perfect abstract complement to the furniture.

Boris Bally, home setting, recycled traffic signs. Photograph: Jeff Johnson. See pages 50-51.

McGovney-Camarot

STEVEN McGOVNEY ■ TAMMY CAMAROT ■ 6585 EAST 6TH STREET #B ■ PRESCOTT VALLEY, AZ 86314
TEL 928-775-8243 ■ FAX 928-775-8248 ■ E-MAIL CONTACT@MCGOVNEYCAMAROT.COM ■ WWW.MCGOVNEYCAMAROT.COM

Top: *Odyssey* teapot and four cups, handpainted, slip-cast ceramic, teapot: 13.5" × 13.5" × 4", cups: 4" × 5" × 3.5".
Bottom: Stemware, crystal with ceramic painted base, 8.5"–10"H. Photograph: Christopher Marchetti.

TIPS FOR AN ARTFUL HOME
Bringing the Outdoors In

Infinitely changeable still-life compositions are one of the most enjoyable ways to integrate sculptural artworks into your home. This ikebana vase encourages playfulness. Its complex sculptural form creates a balance with larger elements in the room and allows for an unending variety of compositions incorporating natural materials. At the same time, the floral and stone arrangement brings nature indoors and softens the masculine aesthetic of the Arts and Crafts chairs.

Carol Green, double-bowl ikebana on handmade table. Photograph: Jim Reem. See page 168.

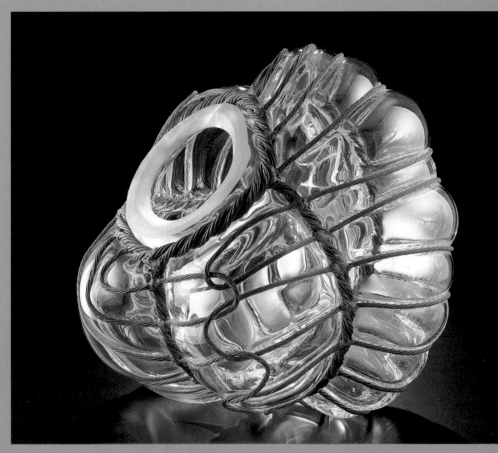

OBJECTS

LYNN EVERETT READ

VITRELUXE GLASS WORKS ■ 639 NORTH BUFFALO STREET ■ PORTLAND, OR 97217 ■ TEL 503-978-0819
E-MAIL LYNNREAD@MSN.COM ■ WWW.VITRELUXE.COM

Top left: *Sellwood Sessions #1 and #2*, 2002, blown glass, left: 16" × 8" × 8", right: 19" × 6.5" × 6.5". Top right: *Pinwheel Vases #1, #2 and #3*, 2002, blown glass, each: 18"-20"H.
Bottom right: *Pinwheel Goblets*, flute, peanut and chalise, 6"-8"H. Bottom left: *Venitians Tall Oval* 13" and *Short Ellipse* 9", 2002, blown glass with silverleaf. Photographs: Paul Foster.

JAMES NOWAK

JAMES NOWAK, INC. ▧ 550 12TH AVENUE ▧ SEATTLE, WA 98122 ▧ TEL 206-329-3914 ▧ FAX 206-329-3915
E-MAIL STUDIO@JAMES-NOWAK.COM ▧ WWW.JAMES-NOWAK.COM

Top left: Dichroic chandelier and blown glass vessels. Right: *Tall Aquarium* on *Bubble* pedestal, 2002, blown glass.
Bottom left: *Hard Aquarium* vase, 2002, blown glass. Photographs: Bruce Carroll.

TALKING TO THE ARTIST
Robert Dane

Turnbull/Boudreau

"Glass is such a seductive material," says Robert Dane, who dates his own seduction back to the late 1970s. Dane was teaching ceramics in Massachusetts, but glass soon won him over.

"One reason glass appeals to me is that the tools and the processes we're using basically haven't changed over the last thousand years. We're living in a techno-industrial society, but we're carrying on this tradition, perpetuating the culture of handmade things. A glass blower from a thousand years ago could sit at my bench today and know exactly what to do."

Dane's earliest sculptures took the form of blown glass eggs, which were divided by a cut plate of glass. Over the years his sculpture grew taller and more complex, culminating in the skyscraping *Timbertotem* series and his most recent work, which combines wood and stone with blown and solid glass. His functional works, from candelabra to goblets, have also evolved in color and form.

The artist's own evolution spans years of working in the studio and learning from colleagues. Another source of inspiration is music. His wife, Jayne, directed a high school music program until 1996, when the couple opened an art gallery on Nantucket. (The Dane Gallery shows ceramics, jewelry, fiber and glass.) And Robert has been studying Afro-Cuban percussion for more than seven years now.

"The music of the community is reflected in my pieces," says Dane, who explains that traditional, folkloric Afro-Cuban music—though not as extreme as freewheeling modern jazz—shares the same spirit of improvisation as glassblowing. "When I'm playing in a group, I respond to what the other musicians are doing to create a whole. Something of that improvisation is found in my hot shop, where I work with three assistants. We all have to respond to each other's movements, timing and actions to create the finished piece."

—Jori Finkel

ROBERT DANE

HEATH BROOK STUDIO ■ 24 WEST MAIN STREET ■ HEATH, MA 01346 ■ TEL/FAX 413-337-5736
E-MAIL RDANEHEATH@AOL.COM ■ WWW.DANEGALLERY.COM

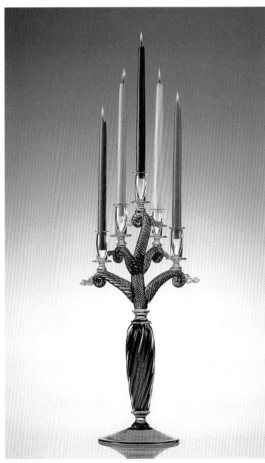

Top: *Tutti Frutti Goblets*, 2002, blown glass, 9"–10"H. Bottom left: *Incalmo Vase*, 2002, blown glass, 16" × 7" × 8".
Bottom right: *Candelabra*, 2002, blown glass, 24" × 10" × 9". Photographs: Paul Turnbull.

DUTCH SCHULZE

BANDON GLASS ART STUDIO ■ 240 HIGHWAY 101 ■ BANDON, OR 97411 ■ TEL 541-347-4723 ■ FAX 541-347-9241
E-MAIL DUTCHARO@DUTCHSCHULZE.COM ■ WWW.DUTCHSCHULZE.COM

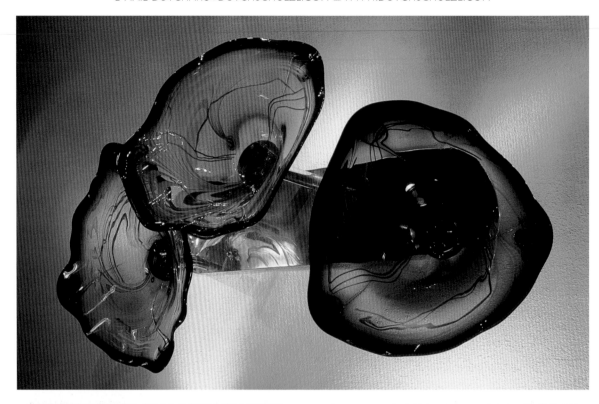

Top: Fluted bowl installation, 2002, blown glass and aluminum, 32" × 65" × 21". Bottom right: Suspended cast glass and steel sculpture, 2002, Texas Tech Medical Center, 15' × 10' × 2'. Bottom left: *The Ruins*, blown and cast glass vessel with lid, 2001, 14" × 9" × 9".

STUDIO PARAN

RICHARD S. JONES ▓ 2051 WINNEBAGO STREET ▓ MADISON, WI 53704 ▓ TEL/FAX 608-242-1111
EMAIL INFO@STUDIOPARAN.COM ▓ WWW.STUDIOPARAN.COM

Top: *Sun Plate*, 2002, handblown glass, 14"Dia. x 2"D. Bottom: *Enso Cylinder Vases*, 2001, handblown glass. Photographs: Jamie Young.

JOSH SIMPSON

JOSH SIMPSON CONTEMPORARY GLASS ▨ 30 FRANK WILLIAMS ROAD ▨ SHELBURNE FALLS, MA 01370
TEL 413-625-6145/413-625-2662 ▨ FAX 413-625-2444 ▨ E-MAIL INFO@MEGAPLANET.COM ▨ WWW.MEGAPLANET.COM

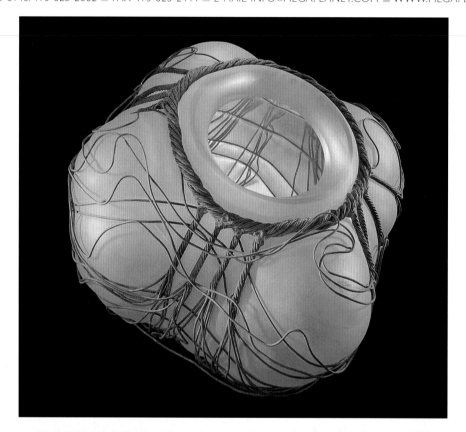

144

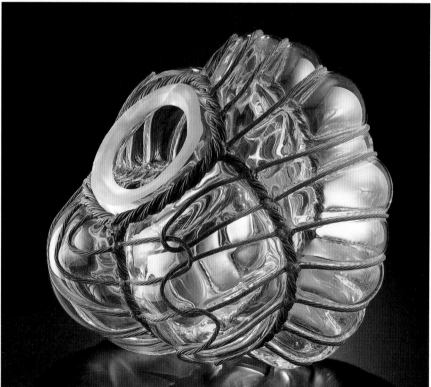

Top: *"Some people can tell what time it is by looking at the sun, but I have never been able to make out the numbers,"*
from the *Copper Baskets* series, blown, sand-blasted glass with sculpted copper wire, 17"L × 16"H × 18"W. Bottom: *"The probability of someone watching over you is*
proportional to the stupidity of your action," from the *Copper Baskets* series, blown glass smith sculpted copper wire, 17"L × 14"H × 15"W. Photographs: Tommy Olof Elder.

TALKING TO THE ARTIST
Josh Simpson

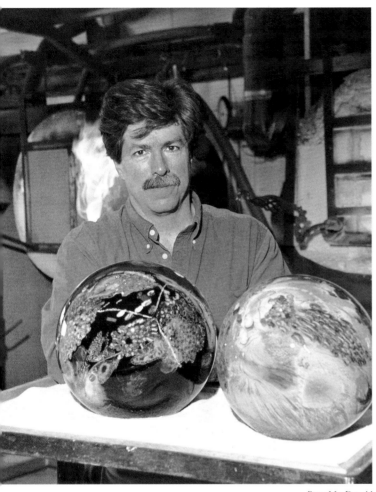

Peter MacDonald

Glass artist Josh Simpson's vision is as vast as the universe, an unlimited landscape that stretches from the mysteries of the ocean to the far reaches of space. Since he began to explore the secrets of his ancient craft more than 30 years ago, Simpson has created a persona every bit as fantastic as his remarkable work.

"I can't say that I had a detailed life plan when I was first captivated by glassblowing, or had any notion of where it would take me," Simpson laughs. "Even now, I never know quite where I'm going until I look back and see the progress."

Self-taught, Simpson used his life savings, which totaled $306, to rent an isolated tract of land in Vermont, hand-build a studio, sew himself an 18-foot cloth tipi to live in, then set about cracking the secret of iridescent Tiffany glass. He succeeded, and then moved on to develop a reputation as one of the foremost contemporary glassblowers in America.

Simpson has become particularly well known for his *Planets.* This evolving series suggests intricately detailed miniature worlds, reminiscent of the rounded shape of the Earth as photographed from space. And if his imaginings about space and the nature of the universe ever grow dim, he can turn to his wife, astronaut Cady Coleman, for firsthand inspiration.

As an extension of his *Planets,* Simpson developed *Megaworlds,* a series of large, heavy glass sculptures. To create a *Megaworld,* Simpson must direct his skilled glass team in a precise, carefully choreographed collaborative effort.

"We look like a bunch of football players trying to do ballet. It's a challenge to control an 80-pound ball of molten glass on the end of a five-foot-long blowpipe; the physics are definitely working against you. My team knows what to do, working through experience and few words. You must be precise and graceful, as well as extremely strong, because the glass is so responsive and alive."

— Susan Troller

SUZANNE CRANE

MUD DAUBER POTTERY ▨ 4225 EARLYSVILLE ROAD ▨ EARLYSVILLE, VA 22936
TEL 434-973-7943 ▨ FAX 434-973-8379 ▨ E-MAIL SUE@SUZANNECRANE.COM ▨ WWW.SUZANNECRANE.COM

146

Top left: Virginia Creeper lamp, 2000, stoneware, 24"H with shade. Top center: Palm Persian platter (detail, 2001), stoneware, 16" × 16" × 2".
Top right: Amber palm candlesticks, 2002, stoneware, 12" × 6" × 6".
Bottom: Footed sink basin and botanical tiles, 2002, stoneware, sink: 7"x17"x17"; tiles: 6"x6". Photographs: Scott Smith.

BILL GOSSMAN

GOSSMAN POTTERY ▨ PO BOX 312 ▨ NEW LONDON, MN 56273 ▨ TEL 320-354-5723
E-MAIL GOSSPOTTERY@TDS.NET ▨ WWW.GEOCITIES.COM/WORLDSBESTPOTTER

Top: *3 Sisters*, 2001, wood-fired stoneware and porcelain, up to 12"H. Bottom: *Firkant*, 1999, wood-fired stoneware, 15"Dia. x 3". Photographs: Peter Lee.

BEN OWEN III

BEN OWEN POTTERY ■ 2199 HIGHWAY 705 SOUTH ■ SEAGROVE, NC 27341 ■ TEL 910-464-2261 ■ FAX 910-464-5444
E-MAIL INFO@BENOWENPOTTERY.COM ■ WWW.BENOWENPOTTERY.COM

148

Top left: *Bottle*, from the *Waterfall* series, 2001, ash glaze on wood-fired porcelain, 18" x 18" x 33".
Top right: *Neolithic Vases*, 2002, salt-glazed stoneware, 22" x 22" x 30" and 11" x 11" x 15".
Bottom: *Faceted Ginger Jar*, 2001, wood-fired stoneware with oribe glaze, 18" x 18" x 24". Photographs: David H. Ramsey.

BEN OWEN III

BEN OWEN POTTERY ■ 2199 HIGHWAY 705 SOUTH ■ SEAGROVE, NC 27341 ■ TEL 910-464-2261 ■ FAX 910-464-5444
E-MAIL INFO@BENOWENPOTTERY.COM ■ WWW.BENOWENPOTTERY.COM

Chinese red dogwood vase, 2001, earthenware, 17" x 17" x 33". Photograph : David H. Ramsey.

LYDIA GREY

156 CHESTNUT HILL ROAD ▩ ORANGE, MA 01364 ▩ TEL 978-544-6264 ▩ E-MAIL LGREY.JAVANET@RCN.COM

Top left: *Elation*, 2001, smoke-fired porcelain, 7.5" x 6.5". Right: *Icarus*, 2001, smoke-fired porcelain, 18" x 10".
Bottom left: *Sliding into a Dream*, 2001, smoke-fired porcelain, 6" x 8". Photographs: Adam Laipson.

TIPS FOR AN ARTFUL HOME
Mixing Up Your Mediums

The tensile strength of forged iron is beautifully illustrated in this original fireplace screen. Set in the large stone wall of this Rocky Mountain home, the fireplace becomes the primary focal point of the room. Stone—like the other familiar craft mediums, fiber, wood, glass, metal and clay—conveys a distinctive character: geological, strong and stable. Fiber and wood are warm and nurturing, while glass is clean and utilitarian, a platform for vivid color. Metal is cool and decorative while clay is elemental and of the earth. Use these materials like paints in your decorative toolbox.

Glenn Gilmore, fireplace doors with stylized grapevine motif. Photograph: McNabb Studios. See pages 92-93.

TOM KENDALL

OAK LEAF POTTERY ■ 10936 THREE MILE ROAD ■ PLAINWELL, MI 49080 ■ TEL 269-664-5430
E-MAIL OAKLEAFPOTTERY@MEI.NET ■ WWW.MEI.NET/~OAKLEAFPOTTERY

Top left: Vase, 2002, porcelain, 24" x 9" x 9". Top right: Vessels, 2002, porcelain, 7" x 13"H. Bottom: Tile panel, 2002, porcelain.

PATRICK JOHNSON

PO BOX 384 ■ 1836 SOUTH ROAD ■ MARLBORO, VT 05344 ■ TEL 802-257-0922 ■ E-MAIL SKYE@SOVER.NET

Top left: *Flights of Fancy*, stoneware, 15" x 11" x 6". Top right: *Galapagos Tortoise with Darwin's Finch*, stoneware, 24" x 22" x 16". Bottom: *Large Hatchling Bowl*, stoneware, 16" x 16" x 5", may also be displayed on the wall. Photographs: Jeff Baird.

LOIS S. SATTLER

LOIS SATTLER CERAMICS ▨ 3620 PACIFIC AVENUE ▨ MARINA DEL RAY, CA 90292-5724 ▨ TEL 310-821-7055 ▨ FAX 310-821-3012
E-MAIL CLAGRLLOIS@AOL.COM

154

Left: Kimono on metal stand with bamboo legs, 2002, black clay, 20"H. Photograph: Bernard Wolf.
Right: Bell on metal stand, 2001, black clay, 25"H. Photograph: Chris Warner.

MARILYN MINTER

STUDIO 12, TORPEDO FACTORY ▧ 105 NORTH UNION STREET ▧ ALEXANDRIA, VA 22314
TEL 703-548-2939/301-424-5134 ▧ E-MAIL SONGSPOTS@COMCAST.NET

 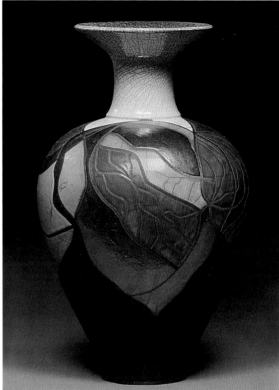

Top left: *Plaid Pot*, 2001, raku clay, 18" x 14". Photograph: P.R.S. Elbo. Top right: *Multicolored Vase*, 2001, raku clay, 18.5" x 14". Photograph: P.R.S. Elbo.
Bottom: *Copper-Lidded Urn*, 2002, raku clay, 9" x 7.5". Photograph: Richard Rodrigues.

EMI OZAWA

21 COVE STREET ▨ NEW BEDFORD, MA 02744 ▨ TEL/FAX 508-990-0041 ▨ E-MAIL EMIOZAWA@EARTHLINK.NET

Top (from left to right): *Seesaw 2*, 2001, apple plywood, acrylic paint and brass, 9" × 19.5" × 8". *Four Quarters*, 2001, cherry, acrylic paint, milk paint and rear earth magnet, 4.5" × 25.5" × 3". *Pendulum Box*, 2001, poplar, acrylic paint and brass, 9.5" × 4.5" × 5.5". *Quack-Quack*, 2000, apple plywood, cherry, milk paint and acrylic paint, 13" × 17" × 5". *Half Moon*, 1999, mahogany, 3.5" × 7" × 3". Bottom: same pieces, opened. Photographs: Mark Johnston.

BINH PHO

WONDERS OF WOOD ■ 48W175 PINE TREE DRIVE ■ MAPLE PARK, IL 60151 ■ TEL 630-365-5462 ■ FAX 630-365-5837
E-MAIL TORIALE@MSN.COM ■ WWW.WONDERSOFWOOD.NET

King and I, 2001, ebonized oak, box elder, pink ivory, acrylic and 22K gold leaf, 18"H x 8"Dia.

THE CHARACTER OF COLOR

Color is a manifestation of light and energy; it transforms the world and deeply affects our outlook on life. Hues are altered in different lights and at different times of the day, and the intensity of a color changes when that color is juxtaposed with elements such as wood, stone and metal. Wherever you live—near the ocean or the desert, in midtown Manhattan or rural Idaho—the environment dictates the intensity and path of light and, thereby, the appearance of color. Architects, like artists, are extremely sensitive to geography, climate and the casting of light; regional styles of architecture have developed, over time, in response to this important sensitivity.

As you cultivate your color palette, think about more than simply the colors you like. Think about color in the context of your environment and the architectural style of your home. Think about the intensity and the path of light in each room throughout the day and in each season. It's a balance with nature that you seek.

Color is the least costly way to transform a room and the single most important influence in creating an appealing environment. Good, personalized color choices will strengthen your personal aesthetic and make it easier to invite art into your home.

One of the ways you can enrich your color palette is to tap into the historical wisdom and common associations of different colors. Keep in mind, as you read what follows, that it is the subtle permutations of color that deepen or lessen its influence on the mood and atmosphere of a room.

White

White represents purity and innocence. Its essence lies in the paradox that its lack of color is its color. This makes it the traditional choice as a background, so that everything around it stands out in contrast. Stark white is cold; it can look almost blue, especially if you live in the mountains where it often snows. Be attentive to the many shades of white; by adding touches of other colors, you can achieve just the right blend to balance the brightness with a feeling of warmth and comfort.

Black

Black creates a sense of intrigue and depth. If applied sparingly, it can be used as an elegant background to highlight framed works of art and set off other colors. For some, its mystery can be magical and sexy, while for others, it feels somber and uncomfortable.

Gray

Hovering somewhere between black and white, gray embodies the properties of transition. Gray is a powerful color, and in combination with white, it has become fashionable as a background color. It reflects a contemporary and modern aesthetic, and works well in combination with other colors; in fact, left alone gray can sometimes appear drab and lonely. Pale shades of gray, such as pearl gray, are very effective in setting off bold and colorful framed art.

Tabletop vases, candlesticks and circular side tables complement the straight lines of the framed wall piece while playing against its strong horizontal presence in this cozy living space. Interior design by Barbara Hauben Ross.

Brown

Brown connects us to our roots. It signals aging, as most things turn a shade of brown over time. Lighter shades of brown, like beige, tan and sand, create an earthy feel, while darker shades can feel murky and foreboding. Brown absorbs glare when mixed with shades of red. It also softens the impact of the sun in environments where the light is harsh and the climate is dry.

Red

Because it is a color of power and passion, red should not be used as a main color in your home. It is best applied sparingly, as an accent, to add a touch of drama. It is a close companion to brown, and together they represent the core of earthy tonality and rustic texture. Shades like terra cotta and coral can be wonderful in environments where your home is rooted in the landscape. Try red in combination with primary blues, greens and yellows when you want a vibrant pop, and consider it for accents such as doors, window frames and trim in a child's or guest's room. Deep, dark reds such as burgundies are excellent complements to dark woods in formal rooms.

Pink

Pink is a calmer shade of red. It's feminine and nurturing, and is known to have sedative qualities. Pink is a favorite hue for bedrooms and children's rooms, where it creates a sense of healing.

Green

Green is the color of nature and growth. It's at the center of the color spectrum and stimulates feelings of harmony and peace. Green is a color of balance; it is highly adaptable and its restful properties make it ideal for use in lighter shades as a neutral or background color. Darker shades like moss or forest absorb glare beautifully.

Blue

Blue is associated with introspection, tranquility and serenity. It also represents the spirit and energy of water. Blue induces sleep and lighter shades, like sky blue, are favorites for use in bedrooms. If you are a lover of blue, study the way the entire blue spectrum is used in Scandinavia, an environment of long, dark winters and sparkling, bright summers.

Purple

Purple is considered an artistic color and is associated with meditation, ritual and spirituality. It is also regal and dignified. Darker shades, like plum, include more red and are thus associated with fire and passion. Lighter shades, like lavender and soft violet, promote a lovely, subtle sense of solitude and reflection in a bedroom, den or library.

Yellow

Yellow represents the power of the sun and is associated with vitality, intellect and longevity. This is a color that's all about energy. Pale, warm shades of yellow, like lemon, are becoming fashionable in dining rooms, where friends and family gather. Darker shades, like saffron and sunflower, are attractive options as accent colors on doors and window trims.

Orange

Orange is a vibrant color often associated with health and wellness. Earthy orange tones have become popular as accents, especially in rooms where the light is misty and the climate is damp. Orange represents optimism and adds a welcoming note to entryways and hallways. It tends to brighten a space, stimulating conversation and ideas. Homes in tropical climates can thrive in the soothing richness of orange.

Zen Stone Furnishings, *Zen Buffet Table, Rock Tower Lamp* and red wall sconce. Photograph: Eric Swanson/The Santa Fe Catalogue. See page 82.

DALE MARHANKA

6904 BARNACK DRIVE ■ SPRINGFIELD, VA 22152 ■ TEL 703-569-4955
E-MAIL DALE.L.MARHANKA@VERIZON.NET

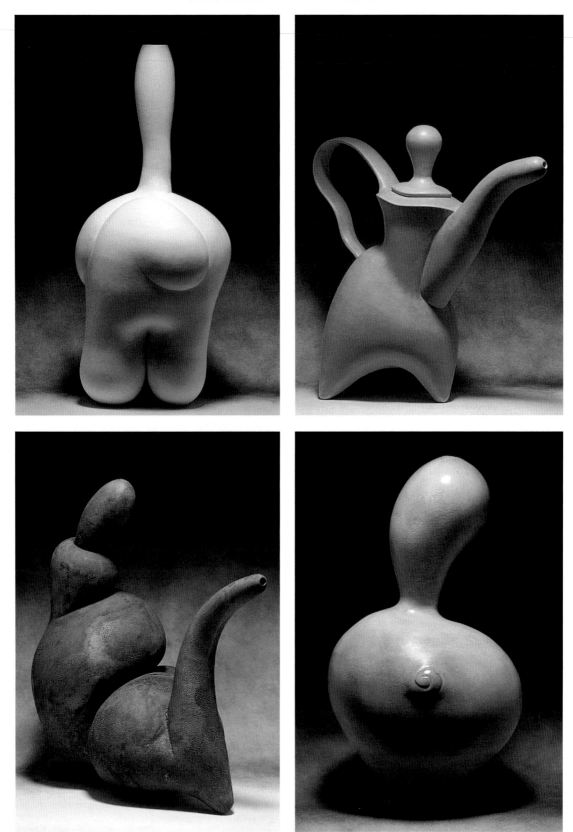

Top left: Vase form, 1999, thrown and altered clay, 21" x 9" x 9". Top right: Teapot, 1999, thrown and altered clay, 15" x 18" x 8".
Bottom right: Vessel, 2001, thrown and altered clay, 19" x 10" x 9". Bottom left: Ewer, 1997, thrown and altered clay, 13" x 12" x 8".

162

ANN MALLORY

201 PAINTER HILL ROAD ■ ROXBURY, CT 06783 ■ TEL/FAX 860-350-3828 ■ E-MAIL AMALLORYDESIGN@EARTHLINK.NET

Top left: *Casing #2*, 2002, ceramic, 29" × 15"Dia. Top right: *Stem with Fruit #2*, 2002, ceramic, 26" × 14"Dia.
Bottom left: *Casing #3*, 2002, ceramic, 27" × 12"Dia. Bottom right: *Casing #1*, 2002, ceramic, 26" × 16"Dia. Photographs: Addison Doty.

DAVID WOODRUFF

WOODRUFF WOODS ■ 192 SONATA DRIVE ■ LEWISVILLE, NC 27023 ■ TEL 866-739-6637 (TOLL FREE)
E-MAIL PDWOODS@TRIAD.RR.COM ■ WWW.PDWOODS.COM

164

Top left: *Nature's Windows* vase, manzanita and ebony, 13" × 7". Top right: Natural-edge vase, white oak and ebony, 12" × 6.5".
Bottom: Rimmed, hollow-formed bowl, oak and ebony, 7" × 13". Photographs: McNabb Studio.

MASUO OJIMA

OJIMA CERAMICS ▨ 2143 WEST 21ST STREET ▨ LOS ANGELES, CA 90018 ▨ TEL 323-734-0723
E-MAIL MOJIMA@EARTHLINK.NET ▨ WWW.OJIMACERAMICS.COM

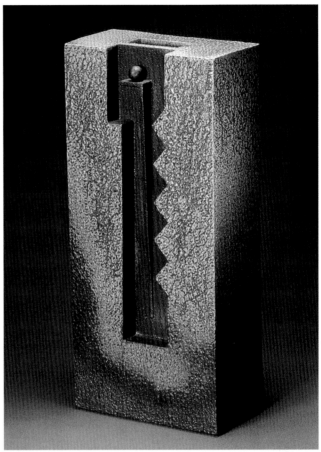

165

Top left: Sculptural vessel, ceramic, 16" × 8" × 8". Top right: *Cityscape* sculptural vessel, ceramic, 25" × 12" × 7".
Bottom: Double-wall bowl, ceramic, 9" × 14" × 14".

6581 FOX RUN ■ SAN ANTONIO, TX 78233 ■ TEL 210-656-8440

166

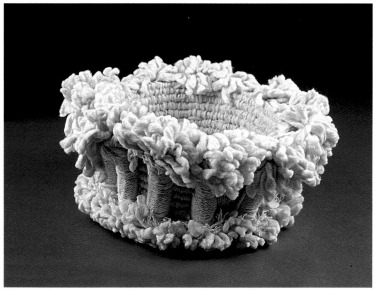

Top: *Parting of the Red Sea*, wool over sisal, 3" x 12" x 7". Bottom: *The Essential Truth*, cotton over fiberflex, 5.5" x 12.5". Photographs: Frank Castillo.

ERIN LAREAU

ERINLAREAU.COM ■ 2645 DESMOND ESTATES ROAD ■ LOS ANGELES, CA 90046 ■ TEL 323-851-9444 ■ FAX 323-851-4810
E-MAIL ERIN@ERINLAREAU.COM ■ WWW.ERINLAREAU.COM

167

Left: *Spinal Tap - Unionjack, 38.* Top right: *Baby Block* (1 of 12), 2".
Middle right: *Music Box,* 6". Bottom right: *Bellamundo,* kinetic globe, 24,000 crystals, 17". Photographs: rich@marchewka.com.

CAROL GREEN

CAROL GREEN STUDIO ■ ELBURN, IL 60119 ■ TEL 630-365-1238 ■ FAX 630-365-1337
E-MAIL CAROL@CAROLGREEN.COM ■ WWW.CAROLGREEN.COM

168

Top: *Single Branch Ikebana,* 2001, cast bronze, copper and patina, 26" x 8" x 11". Bottom: *Double Bowl Ikebana,* 2002, cast bronze and patina, 29" x 7" x 23". Photographs: Jim Reem.

SCULPTURE

ATELIER BALL

HIRAM BALL ■ 518 ACADEMY AVENUE ■ SEWICKLEY, PA 15143 ■ TEL 724-266-1502 ■ FAX 724-266-1504
E-MAIL BALL@BALL-CONSULTING-LTD.COM ■ WWW.ATELIERBALL.COM

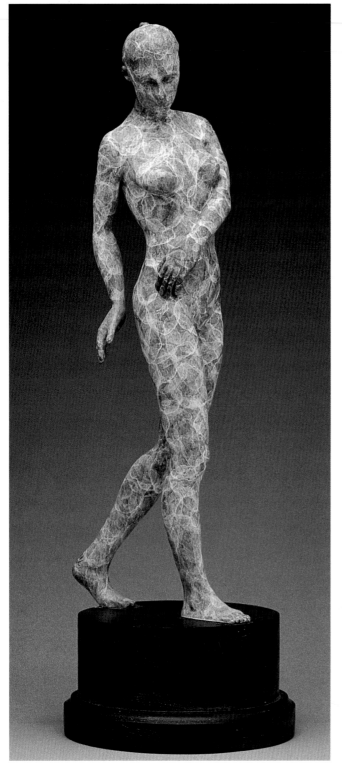

Left: *La Femme Rytmique I*, 2001, bronze, 23" x 5" x 5".
Top right: *Ray of Hope*, 2000, bronze, 28" x 21" x 5". Bottom right: *Seated Torso*, 1996, bronze, 24" x 10" x 10". Photographs: Jaffe Parsons.

CHAD AWALT

AWALT WOODCARVING AND DESIGN ■ 4731 STERLING ACRES COURT ■ TUCKER, GA 30084
TEL 770-493-1750 ■ FAX 770-493-1975 ■ E-MAIL AWALT@MINDSPRING.COM ■ WWW.CHADAWALT.COM

Vetumnus, hand-carved linden wood, 34" x 20" x 14". Photograph: Neil Dent.

BRUMDER FINE ART

POLLY BRUMDER ▥ 3476 IRIS COURT ▥ BOULDER, CO 80304 ▥ TEL 303-440-6473 ▥ FAX 303-413-1792
E-MAIL BRUMDERSCULPTURE@YAHOO.COM

172

Maya's Gift, 2002, bronze, 29" x 13" x 12".

CHARIS CONGAIL

CONGAIL STUDIOS ▓ 1331 CEAPE AVENUE ▓ OSHKOSH, WI 54901
TEL 920-235-7236 ▓ E-MAIL CONGAILSTUDIOS@HOTMAIL.COM

Top left: *Pensive*, gypsum, 15" × 8" × 11.5". Right: *Jory Ayer*, gypsum, 18.5" × 8.5" × 10".
Bottom left: *Dan Earle*, gypsum, 16.5" × 8.5" × 9". Photographs: Paul Malmquist.

JIM LICARETZ

IDOLLATRY INC. ▉ 1125 SOUTH GAFFEY STREET ▉ SAN PEDRO, CA 90731 ▉ TEL 310-832-6993 ▉ FAX 310-832-6993
E-MAIL IDOLLS@EARTHLINK.NET ▉ WWW.JIMLICARETZ.COM

174

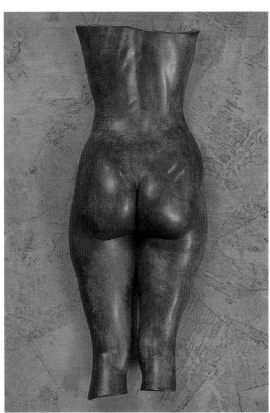

Top left: *Hommage à l'antiquitè No. 1*, 2001, bronze, 24" x 7" x 3". Top right: *Memoire de l'antiquitè No. 1*, 2002, bronze, 28" x 11" x 8".
Bottom left: *Hommage à l'antiquitè No. 2*, 2001, bronze, 17" x 7" x 3". Bottom right: *Memoire de l'antiquitè No. 2*, 2002, bronze, 28" x 11" x 8".

GERALD SICILIANO

STUDIO DESIGN ASSOCIATES ■ 9 GARFIELD PLACE ■ BROOKLYN, NY 11215 ■ TEL/FAX 718-636-4561
E-MAIL GSSTUDIO@CONCENTRIC.NET ■ WWW.GERALDSICILIANOSTUDIO.COM ■ WWW.CONCENTRIC.NET/~GSSTUDIO

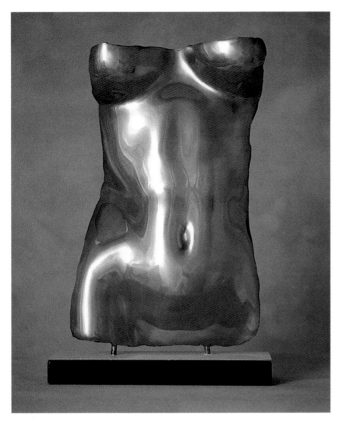

175

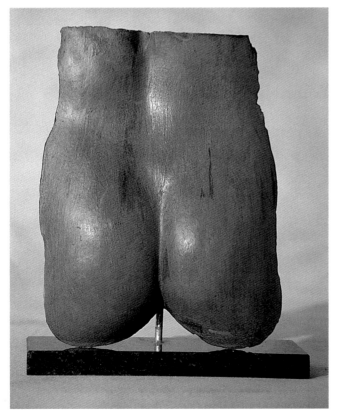

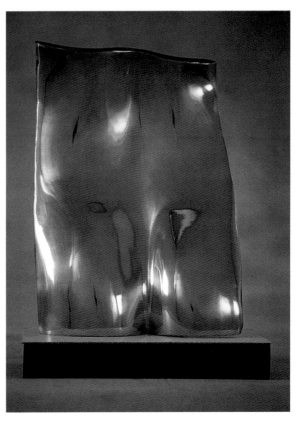

Top left: *Torso*, bronze, 15" × 10" × 3.5". Top right: *Mezza Chiappa*, patinated bronze, 12.25" × 8" × 3.5".
Bottom left: *Chiappa Bella*, polychromed terra cotta, 12" × 9" × 3.5". Bottom right: *Chaip*, polished bronze, 10.25" × 8" × 3.5".

TALKING TO THE ARTIST
Gwenn Connolly

Gwenn Connolly's vibrant bronze sculpture makes abstractions like energy, spirit and possibility visible in three dimensions. Her work fairly dances with the pleasure and potential of being human as it celebrates the powerful grace of the animated figure.

"I work primarily with the female figure, and I'm interested in exploring ideas, emotions and the power and strength of the

Arthur Stern

human spirit. Although the shapes I create are very elongated, linear human forms, they are not fragile at all. People tell me how much strength they see in my work."

These feminine shapes take enormous strides on elongated toes, swing from the moon and appear capable of dancing across the world in a single joyful leap. Their bodies and gestures are a compelling combination of highly expressive abstraction and exuberant sexuality. Ranging in size from tabletop to larger-than-life, these bronze figures hardly seem like objects, so possessed are they of energy and movement.

Connolly attended San Francisco State University, the Mendocino Art Center and the Academy of Art in San Francisco, where she received a bachelor of fine arts degree.

Today Connolly lives and works in Benicia, California, an hour outside of San Francisco. Her sculpture is represented in dozens of private collections, and she has had many exhibitions in the Bay Area and in states outside of California. She has a studio in a complex that houses other artists and enjoys being part of a vigorous, supportive arts community.

"When I begin a new piece, there's a period of infatuation. It's like falling in love; I am passionately involved with it every waking moment. Then, like in a relationship, the infatuation passes and the hard work begins. I have to begin solving problems and making decisions necessary to bring the piece to fulfillment. It's fascinating and sometimes frustrating, but always rewarding when a sculpture is completed."

—Susan Troller

GWENN CONNOLLY

PO BOX 1781 ■ BENICIA, CA 94510 ■ TEL 707-747-1822
E-MAIL GWENNART1@AOL.COM ■ WWW.CONNOLLY-SCULPTURE.COM

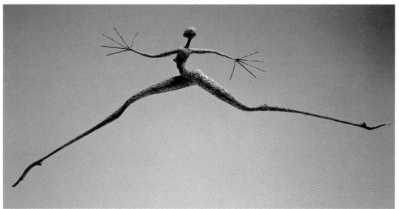

Top: *Dancer*, 4.4'H × 2.25'W × 3.3'D. Bottom: *Leap of Faith*, 3.75'H × 9.25'W × 1'D.

DANIEL B. GLANZ

DANIEL GLANZ STUDIOS ■ 3496 WHITETAIL CIRCLE ■ WELLINGTON, CO 80549
TEL 970-690-8425 ■ E-MAIL GLANZSTUDIOS@MSN.COM ■ WWW.GLANZSCULPTURES.COM

Top left: *Dancer III*, bronze, 40" x 23". Top right: *Aurora's Path*, bronze, 19" x 19". Bottom: *After the Hunt*, bronze, 15" x 23". Photographs: Jafe Parsons.

MARK HOPKINS SCULPTURE, INC.

MARK HOPKINS ■ 21 SHORTER INDUSTRIAL BOULEVARD ■ ROME, GA 30165 ■ TEL 706-235-8773 ■ FAX 706-235-2814
E-MAIL MARKHOPKINSSCULPTURE@WEBACCESS.NET ■ WWW.MARKHOPKINSSCULPTURE.COM

Top: *Mud Buddies*, bronze, 16" x 35". Bottom left: *Wyatt*, bronze, 18" x 15". Bottom right: *Day Break*, bronze, 22" x 41".

DAVID L. HOSTETLER

WINTER TEL 740-593-8180 ■ SUMMER: HOSTETLER GALLERY ■ #2 OLD SOUTH WHARF ■ PO BOX 2222 ■ NANTUCKET, MA 02584
TEL 508-228-3117/508-228-5152 ■ E-MAIL HOSTETLER@EUREKANET.COM ■ WWW.DAVIDHOSTETLER.COM

Top left: *Duo*, bronze with blue-green patina, 38.5" × 12" × 7", edition of 15.
Top right: *Sensuous Woman*, bronze with brown-gold patina, total: 65"H (base: 18"H), edition of 15. Bottom right: *Asherah Tree Goddess*,
bronze with pale gray-beige patina, 46"H, edition of 15. Bottom left: *Seated Woman*, ginko wood and paint, 49"H. Photographs: Lyntha Scott Eiler.

SEYMOUR L. SHUREN

983 HAVERSTRAW ROAD ▧ WESLEY HILLS, NY 10901 ▧ TEL/FAX 845-354-8996
E-MAIL SSHURENINC@AOL.COM ▧ WWW.SSHURENINC.COM

Top left: *Meditation*, dense white alabaster, 21"H × 17"W × 11"D. Top right: *Waves*, sungold alabaster, 21"H × 16"W × 14"D.
Bottom left: *Merlin*, Arcobaleno alabaster, 17"H × 12"W × 12"D. Bottom right: *Tranquility*, Portugese pink marble, 22"H × 12"W × 7"D. Photographs: Howard Goodman.

DETERMINING VALUE

Let's face it. When we find artwork that appeals to us, our reaction is likely to be subjective and immediate. We fall in love with it first—and *then* think about the pragmatic aspects of buying or owning it.

But before you buy that sculpture or handmade table, it's important to ask some hard-nosed questions. Do I want to live with this work for years to come? If I buy it, where will I place it? And, equally important: is the piece worth the asking price?

Here at GUILD, we help thousands of customers purchase original art each year. We also interact with hundreds of artists. Based on what we've learned, we can suggest some guidelines for assessing the value of a work of art.

COST AND VALUE

One criterion that all experts and collectors will agree on is this: buy art that you love. If you love it and can afford it, many say, you should buy it; all other considerations are secondary. While we agree with the spirit of this suggestion, we also think you'll make better and more confident purchases if you conduct basic research into the artist's background and stature.

Pricing

The cost of a work of art is often related to the experience of the artist. Those who have worked in their fields for many years command higher prices than relative newcomers. The same is true for artists whose work is included in museum collections or publications, or who have mounted one-person shows. These are landmark events; they demonstrate respect for the artist on the part of curators, publishers and gallery managers, and they have a cumulative effect on the artist's prices.

Whether or not a work of art seems expensive, it's good to remember that value and price are different qualities. The value of artwork is perceived and subjective, while the price is set and, usually, firm.

Education

An artist's academic record sheds more light on his technical background and skills than his natural talent. Museums and institutions consider an artist's schooling important, particularly when selecting emerging artists to participate in shows. Your choice of a glass vase or garden sculpture, however, should not be based on which institution granted the artist a master's degree—or even whether the artist holds that degree. Some of our most esteemed artists developed their skills as apprentices or within an artists' community rather than at an institution.

History of Exhibitions

More than schooling, an artist's credibility is reflected in the number and range of shows that have exhibited his work. This is a very important reference point for value. Young artists compete to participate in group shows at local and regional galleries. Artists who are more advanced in their careers mount one-person shows. Exhibitions give artists an opportunity to obtain exposure and gauge the response to their work.

Opposite: Playful tabletop sculptures soften the hard, predictable lines of the furniture and windows in this beautiful living space designed by Mary Drysdale. Photograph: Andrew Lautman.

THE VALUE OF PASSION

Although the factors discussed here relate to marketplace value, they should also be considered as you think about the value an artwork has for you and your family. That said, we couldn't emphasize too strongly that your passion for a work of art should always drive your purchase.

Buying art for your home involves a different set of standards than those faced by a major collector or museum. The right surroundings and appropriate placement in your home environment are much more important than investment appeal or a history of shows at major museums. Original art has an aesthetic and emotional impact on your home.

This is one area where it's important to lead with your heart.

When reviewing an artist's resume, pay close attention to the dates and locations of exhibitions.

- How long has the artist been exhibiting?
- Has the work been exhibited regionally, nationally or internationally?
- Are the exhibition sites well known?
- Has the artist received any awards?

Editorial Reviews

Reviews in journals, magazines and newspapers are another benchmark of value. Art critics act as interpreters, and their exhibition reviews not only evaluate the quality of artworks, but also place them in the context of history and genre. A strong endorsement by a respected critic can have a significant influence on an artist's career.

Collections

It can be interesting to learn which private, public and corporate collections include works by a particular artist, and if you're interested in acquiring the work of an emerging artist, it's affirming to learn that others share that passion. With established artists, it becomes substantially more important to know who owns their work. If the work is part of a museum collection, for example, this adds to the value. Likewise, ownership by collectors and corporations can have a significant influence on price.

Career Overview

Artists go through periods of development influenced by the world around them, producing work around particular techniques and themes of influence. When you meet artists or gallery curators, ask them to comment on the artist's body of work. How long has the artist been developing a particular theme or using a specific technique? How refined are the themes and techniques? Is the artist highly prolific? The answers to these questions will provide insight into the artist's depth of experience; in that way, they may influence the value you place on the work.

BILL HOPEN

HOPEN STUDIO INC. ▪ 227 A MAIN STREET ▪ SUTTON, WV 26601 ▪ TEL 304-765-5611/800-872-8578
E-MAIL HOPEN@MOUNTAIN.NET ▪ WWW.AAGG.COM/HOPEN

Top: *Originals*, lost wax bronze, 8"H. Center: Selection of cast crystal and bronze. Bottom: *Appalachian Dance* series, bronze, 5"H, limited editions. Photographs: Jurgin Lorenzen.

CAROLE A. FEUERMAN

FEUERMAN STUDIOS, INC. ■ 350 WARREN STREET ■ JERSEY CITY, NJ 07302 ■ TEL 201-432-9200 ■ FAX 201-432-1202
E-MAIL CAROLJF@MINDSPRING.COM ■ WWW.FEUERMAN-STUDIOS.COM

186

World on 9/11/01, 2001, bronze, 42" sphere. Photograph: Dan Morgan.

DANI

15619 INDIAN HEAD COURT ■ RAMONA, CA 92065 ■ TEL 760-787-9813 ■ FAX 760-787-9814 ■ E-MAIL DANI1001@AOL.COM

Left: *Ethereal*, bronze, 34"H. Right: *Lotus Blossom*, bronze, 23"H.

ALAN LeQUIRE

ALAN LeQUIRE, SCULPTOR ■ 4304 CHARLOTTE AVENUE SUITE C ■ NASHVILLE, TN 37209 ■ TEL/FAX 615-298-4611
E-MAIL LEQUIRE@MINDSPRING.COM ■ WWW.ALANLEQUIRE.COM

188

Left: *Athena Parthenos*, 1982-2002, Nashville, TN, gypsum, fiberglass and steel, 42'H. Top right: *Timothy Demontbrun*, 1996, Nashville, TN, bronze, heroic scale.
Bottom right: *Jess*, 1997, bronze, life size. Photograph: John Guider.

189

Top: *Jackson's Chameleon*, 1996, mixed media, 18" x 12" x 3".
Bottom: *Gaia: Earth Godess*, 1999, hand-painted ceramic, 28" x 18" x 7". Inset: *Gaia: Earth Godess* (back view).

LINDA M. LEVITON

LINDA LEVITON SCULPTURE ■ 1011 COLONY WAY ■ COLUMBUS, OH 43235
E-MAIL GUILD@LINDALEVITON.COM ■ WWW.LINDALEVITON.COM

190

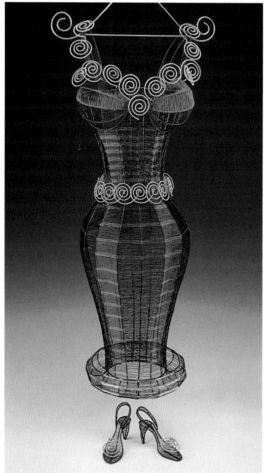

Top: *Eve's Striped Slippers*, copper and brass wire and found objects, variation on size 8 shoe. Bottom left: *Eve in Spirals*, copper and brass wire, total size: 74" x 24" x 13". Bottom right: *Eve on the Vine*, copper and brass wire, total size: 77" x 25" x 18". Photographs: Jerry Anthony.

MARK A. WALLIS

MAW STUDIO ▦ RR 5 BOX 106 ▦ SPENCER, IN 47460
TEL 812-829-1747 ▦ FAX 812-829-3674 ▦ E-MAIL SCULPT45@BLUEMARBLE.NET

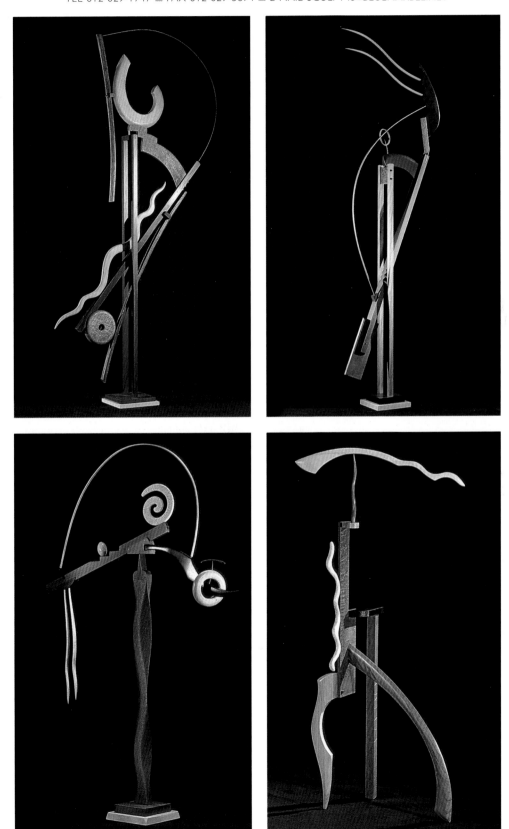

Top left: *A Jazz Noise*, 1996, wood, paint and stone, 12" × 36" × 102". Top right: *Mystical Polarities*, 2000, wood, paint and stone, 12" × 24" × 102".
Bottom left: *Balancing Act*, 2001, mixed woods, paint and graphite, 12" × 54" × 84". Bottom right: *The Player*, 2001, mixed woods and paint, 10" × 24" × 52". Photographs: Spectrum Studio.

ANNIE PASIKOV

360 LONE STAR ROAD ■ LYONS, CO 80540 ■ TEL 303-823-6757 ■ FAX 303-823-8033
E-MAIL PASIKOV@EMAIL.COM ■ WWW.STONESCULPTURES.NET

192

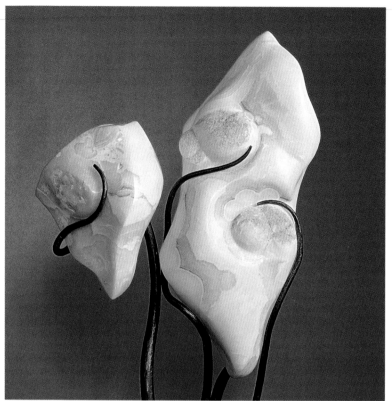

Left: *Awaiting the Dawn*, 2001, bronze cast from marble sculpture, 47", edition of 21. Photograph: Marie Commiskey
Top right: *Reunion*, (detail of 68" sculpture), 2001, onyx on steel. Photograph: Marie Commiskey,
Bottom right: *Mother Earth*, 2000, marble, 24" x 20" x 10". Photograph: Joseph Amram.

ROB FISHER SCULPTURE

ROB FISHER ▧ 228 NORTH ALLEGHENY STREET ▧ BELLEFONTE, PA 16823 ▧ TEL 814-355-1458 ▧ FAX 814-353-9060
E-MAIL GLENUNION@AOL.COM ▧ WWW.SCULPTURE.ORG/PORTFOLIO

193

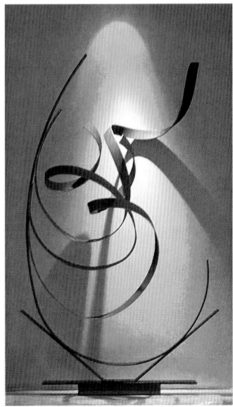

Left: *Chambered Nautilus,* 2002, private residence, Palm Desert, CA, painted steel and anodized aluminum. Top right: *Chambered Nautilus* (detail). Bottom right: *Chambered Nautilus* (detail). Photographs: Courtesy of Andrea Schwartz Gallery, San Francisco, CA.

DEMETRIOS & EAMES

PO BOX 870 ▨ PETALUMA, CA 94953 ▨ TEL 707-769-1777 ▨ FAX 707-769-1780

194

Top left: *Titans*, 2001, bronze, 15" x 9" x 5", artist: L. Demetrios. Photograph: M. Lee Fatherree. Top right: *Star Dance*, steel, gate: 84" x 88" x 2", panel: 44"x 44" x 2", artist: L. Eames.
Bottom right: *Billet Doux*, 1999, bronze, 16.75" x 15.5" x 15.5", artist: L. Eames. Photograph: M. Lee Fatherree.
Bottom left: *Inner Core Sample, VII*, 1999, bronze, 37" x 20" x 16", artist: L. Demetrios. Photograph: M. Lee Fatherree.

JOËL URRUTY

15 MONTGOMERY STREET ■ MIDDLETOWN, NY 10940
TEL/FAX 845-342-2239 ■ E-MAIL INFO@JOELURRUTY.COM ■ WWW.JOELURRUTY.COM

195

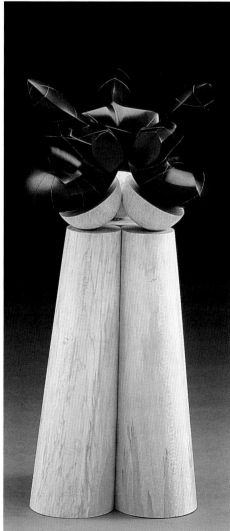

Top: *We*, 2002, mahogany, oak and milkpaint, 20" x 21" x 8". Bottom left: *Three Suns*, 2002, mahogany, sycamore and milkpaint, 27" x 10" x 9".
Bottom right: *Totem*, 2002, mahogany, oak and milkpaint, 26" x 6" x 8". Photographs: Pat Simione.

RAIN HARRIS

1502 SOUTH BROAD STREET ■ PHILADELPHIA, PA 19146 ■ TEL 215-462-6864/215-755-5984 ■ FAX 215-462-8850
E-MAIL RAINBOTPOT@AOL.COM

196

Top: *Vineal*, 2001, stoneware, luster and rhinestones, 22" x 16" x 8". Bottom: *Unfolding Curl*, 2001, stoneware and flocking, 24" x 14" x 10". Photographs: John Carlano.

MARY FISCHER

601 HARMON HILLS ROAD ▨ DRIPPING SPRINGS, TX 78620 ▨ TEL 512-858-4781

197

Top: *Which Way*, 2002, clay, houses: 3" × 3" × 4"; trees: 4.25" × .5"Dia.; base: 15.5" × 3.75" × 1".
Bottom: *Meso American*, 2002, clay, 19" × 3.5" × 15.5". Photographs: Seale Studios, San Antonio, TX.

STEPHAN J. COX

W8651 690TH AVENUE ■ RIVER FALLS, WI 54022 ■ TEL 715-425-7006 ■ FAX 715-425-6668
E-MAIL COXGLASS@PRESSENTER.COM

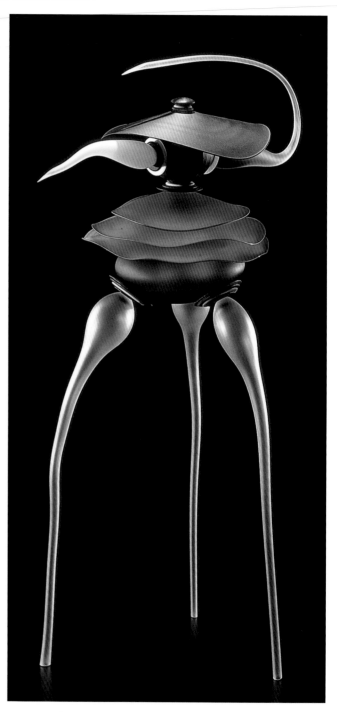

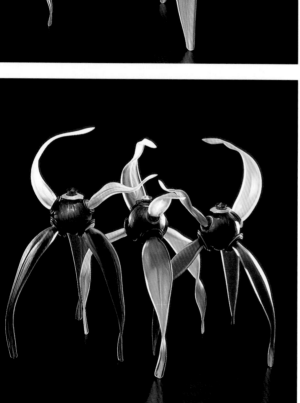

Top left: *Red Leaf Pod*, 2002, glass, 24" × 22" × 22". Right: *Black Hat Teapot*, 2001, glass, 32" × 19" × 12".
Bottom left: *Teapot Group*, 2002, glass, each: 16" × 12" × 12". Photographs: Don Pitlik.

TALKING TO THE ARTIST
Stephan J. Cox

Although he is working at the top of a competitive glass field and has exhibited widely around the world, Stephan J. Cox prefers to keep his studio small.

"I personally design and make every piece of glass. My wife runs the business end of our studio, which is at our home outside of River Falls, Wisconsin. This scale operation has been successful for us and suits what I am trying to do."

Cox began blowing glass in the late 1970s. "I'd attended the University of Minnesota off and on and had worked a series of nasty jobs. Eventually I found my way to the University of Wisconsin–River Falls, where I gravitated toward painting and printmaking, spending most of my time working in the basement print shop. The glass shop was next door, and I found myself drawn to that hot, high-energy environment. The tricky molten material took over my life in 1979, and since then it's been all glass."

"When I began to master some of the techniques, I realized that an obsession with the craft itself can become a trap. When you are single-mindedly trying to reproduce something that is merely mechanically challenging, the emphasis on method can kill your creativity. Craft is vitally important, but it has its place within any art form."

Cox's work is an ongoing study of the interplay between form, color, texture and light. After deciding on the overall form or shape of a piece, Cox chooses his colors. When the form and color are realized, he often adds texture and alters the reflective properties of the piece by carving the blown and cooled glass with various abrasive tools.

"Above all, I love the 'frozen moment' I can achieve with molten glass. Managing that graceful fluidity is a challenge that continues to fascinate me."

— Susan Troller

Jane Lasar

ELIZABETH RYLAND MEARS

WINDY HILL GLASSWORKS ■ 10160 HAMPTON ROAD ■ FAIRFAX STATION, VA 22039-2722 ■ TEL 703-690-2545
E-MAIL ELIZWNDHIL@AOL.COM ■ WWW.WINDYHILLGLASSWORKS.COM

200

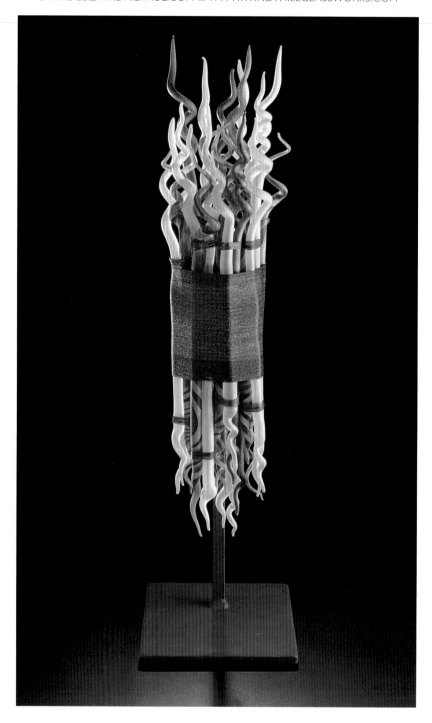

Bundle of Twigs, 2002, glass and mixed media, 18" x 5" x 4". Photograph: Tommy Olof Elder.

VINCENT LEON OLMSTED

613 CLEMON'S AVENUE #1 ■ MADISON, WI 53704 ■ TEL 608-242-7129 ■ E-MAIL VENT123@AOL.COM

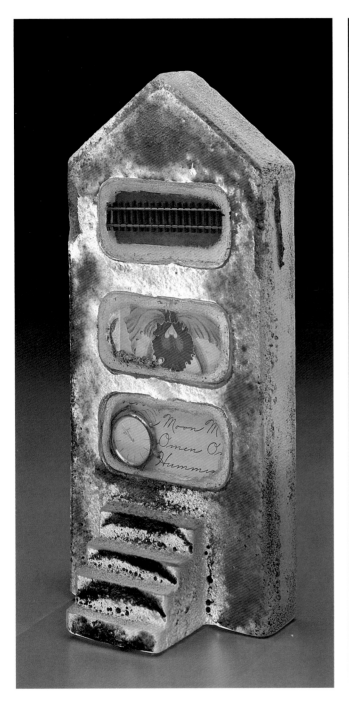 

Taking a Fast Train Down a Wrong Piece of Track (front and back view), 2001, cast glass and found objects, 12" x 6" x 6". Photographs: James Wildman.

THE ROOMS OF YOUR HOME
The Bedroom

A bedroom should be a quiet haven for intimacy and reflection. It's also the perfect setting for creating mood and atmosphere. The color palette should be calm and soothing, with sources of light and sound dimmed and softened at the end of the day. Since the bedroom is a private space, it invites experimentation and expressiveness.

As you think about artworks for the bedroom, begin by considering the bed itself. Furniture makers will be happy to show you photographs of bed frames made for previous clients or discuss a unique design specifically for you. Bedside tables, lamps and wall sconces are also special when made by an artist. Like wood, fiber is very much at home in a bedroom. Tapestries or art quilts can create a strong visual impact and provide a practical benefit by softening sounds.

The bedroom is particularly well suited for art that has strong personal meaning. Many collectors place favorite paintings or objects in the bedroom so they can enjoy them first thing in the morning and last thing at night. Others like to use bedroom walls for black-and-white photographs that invite the eye to relax and encourage contemplative thoughts.

Above: Diana Harrison, *Large Angels Trumpet*, hanging light fixtures. Photograph: John Harkey. See pages 13, 83 and 87.

PINKWATER GLASS

KURT SWANSON ▪ LISA SCHWARTZ ▪ 187 CHURCH HILL ROAD ▪ CARMEL, NY 10512
TEL/FAX 845-225-1057 ▪ E-MAIL PINKWATERGLASS@AOL.COM ▪ WWW.PINKWATERGLASS.COM

Top left: *King Fish*, 2002, handblown glass, 33" x 11" x 8". Top right: *Bird Talk*, 2002, handblown glass, 28" x 20" x 10".
Bottom: Hanging lamps (small), handblown glass, cone: 6" x 8", dome: 8" x 5", tulip: 6" x 6", available in 12 colors. Photographs: Bob Barrett Photography.

TALKING TO THE ARTIST
Jeremy Cline

During the Loma Prieta earthquake of 1989, Jeremy Cline was an art student in San Francisco—and was working in a glass studio at the time. "I was running upstairs to the classroom, blowpipe in hand, when I literally bounced off one wall, and then another. I assumed I had tripped, but when I got to the classroom, everyone looked stunned. 'Did you feel that?' they asked. 'What?' I said. 'Let's blow some glass.'"

Now, more than a decade later, Cline runs his own glass studio in San Francisco with some of the same resistance—even obliviousness—to obstacles. He opened Incline Glass in 1992, fresh from training in Murano, Italy, with glass master Pino Signoretto.

Cline's leading clients thus far have been small lighting companies that manufacture high-end work for restaurants and hotels. But now, with business humming along, Cline wants to carve out more personal time for creating glass sculptures such as his *Birds of Paradise* series.

It was just under six years ago that Cline created his first *Bird of Paradise* sculpture: a full-bodied stalk of glass that tapered at its head and measured 28 inches. More recent examples—done in wild reds, greens and yellows—have reached six feet in height.

Cline created his first *Bird* out of the remains of a commissioned piece. "One day in my studio I noticed the colored pieces that were leftovers from lamps I had been making," he recalls. "I felt inspired that day to combine the pieces in a different way. I usually like straight pieces, symmetrical forms, but in this case I really let the glass tell me what to do. I followed the glass to a new form." And, one could add, to the next stage in his career.

—Jori Finkel

Latchezar Boyadjiev

JEREMY R. CLINE

INCLINE GLASS ■ 768 DELANO AVENUE ■ SAN FRANCISCO, CA 94112 ■ TEL 415-469-8312 ■ FAX 415-469-8463
E-MAIL JC@JEREMYCLINE.COM ■ WWW.JEREMYCLINE.COM

Left: *Birds of Paradise*, blown glass, 60.5" x 11"; 61" x 11.25".
Top right: *Birds of Paradise*, blown glass, 61" x 12"; 57.5" x 12". Bottom right: *Birds of Paradise*, blown glass, 55.5" x 12". Photographs: Latchezar Boyadjiev.

206

CLIFF LEE

170 WEST GIRL SCOUT ROAD ■ STEVENS, PA 17578 ■ TEL 717-733-9373 ■ FAX 717-738-4843

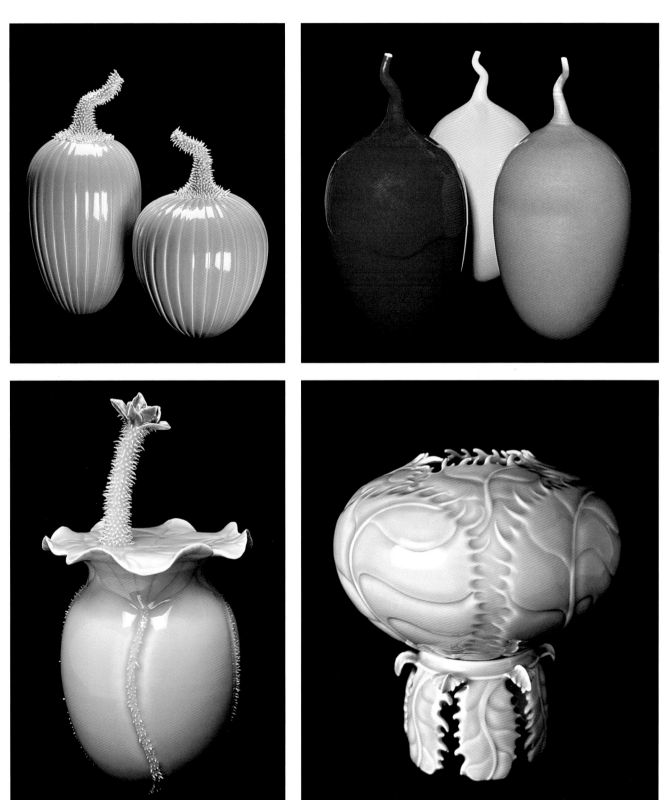

Top left: *Yellow Prickly Melon* vases, 13.5" x 7.5" and 11" x 6.5". Top right: *Trio* (yellow, red, blue) porcelain vases, 14" x 8" and 14.5" x 7.75".
Bottom right: *Cabbage* vase on pedestal, celadon and porcelain, 11" x 7.5". Bottom left: *Lotus* vase, celadon and porcelain, 10.5" x 5.5". Photographs: Holly Lee.

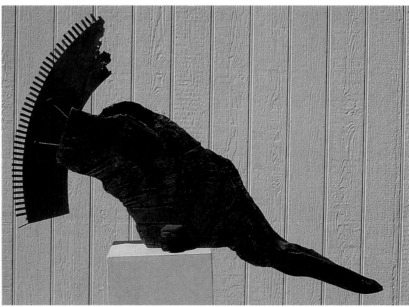

Top: *Point of Balance,* wood and mixed media, 64" x 15" x 10".
Bottom left: *My Devotion,* wood and mixed media, 23" x 15" x 9". Bottom right: *Night Bird,* wood and steel, 63" x 36" x 16".

GARDEN SCULPTURE

RAIN KIERNAN

94 BIRCH HILL ROAD ■ WESTON, CT 06883 ■ TEL 203-226-5045 ■ FAX 203-227-3187
E-MAIL RAIN@RAINKIERNAN.COM ■ WWW.RAINKIERNAN.COM

Top: *Eshe*, 1999, marble, 34" x 42" x 23". Photograph: Patrick Vingo.
Bottom: *Maya*, 2001, marble and brushed stainless steel, 40" x 60" x 41". Photograph: Erin Kiernan.

KAREN HEYL

907 SONIA PLACE ■ ESCONDIDO, CA 92026 ■ TEL 760-489-7106 ■ 1310 PENDLETON STREET ■ CINCINNATI, OH 45202
TEL 513-421-9791 ■ E-MAIL HEYLSTONE2@AOL.COM

Top left: *In the Garden*, 2002, limestone, 36" × 8" × 4". Top right: *Snake in the Grass*, 2002, limestone, 53" × 10" × 2".
Bottom left: *The Couple*, 2002, limestone, 36" × 6" × 3" and 36" × 5" × 5". Bottom right: *On Water's Edge*, 2002, limestone, 27" × 17" × 2". Photographs: Charles Behlow.

ROSETTA

405 EIGHTH STREET SE #15 ▧ LOVELAND, CO 80537 ▧ TEL/FAX 970-667-6265
E-MAIL ROSETTASCULPTURE@EARTHLINK.NET ▧ WWW.ROSETTASCULPTURE.COM

Top: *Mountain Fishing*, 1996, bronze, 29" x 65" x 26". Bottom: *Seated Cheetahs*, 1999, bronze, 50" x 27" x 17". Photographs: Mel Schockner.

ANAHATA ARTS

ERIC DAVID LAXMAN ▓ 478 MOUNTAINVIEW AVENUE ▓ VALLEY COTTAGE, NY 10989 ▓ TEL 845-353-8521 ▓ FAX 845-348-3687
E-MAIL ERIC@ANAHATA.COM ▓ WWW.ANAHATA.COM

213

Top left: *Anahata Fountain,* 2000, private collection, welded silicon bronze, 96" x 36" x 36". Photograph: Stuart Sachs.
Top right: Custom stair railing, 2001, patinated welded steel, 36" x 120"; *Sunflower Lingam* (landing), 1998, marble and steel, 48" x 10" x 10"; *The Inner "I",* 1997, marble and steel,
60" x 15" x 15". Photographs: Sal Cordaro. Bottom: *Serpiente Grande,* 2002, private collection, welded stainless steel, 50' x 27" x 15". Photograph: Eric David Laxman.

CHRISTIANSEN–ARNER

CHERIE CHRISTIANSEN ■ FRANZ ARNER ■ BOX 770 ■ MENDOCINO, CA 95460
TEL/FAX 707-937-3309 ■ WWW.CHRISARNSCULPTURE.COM

214

Left: *Singing Goddess*, 2000, black granite, 6' × 4'. Top right: *Heaven and Earth*, 1997, white granite, labradoite and California jade, 7' × 7.5' × 2'. Bottom right: *Offering*, white granite, California jade and black granite, 5' × 2.5'.

GARY SLATER

SLATER SCULPTURE ▨ 619 SOUTH HACIENDA DRIVE SUITE 6 ▨ TEMPE, AZ 85281 ▨ TEL 480-921-1909 ▨ FAX 480-446-8628
E-MAIL GARY@SLATERSCULPTURE.COM ▨ WWW.SLATERSCULPTURE.COM

Top: *Desert Mountain I*, copper, 4'H × 8'L. Bottom right: *Desert Wave I*, copper, 8'H × 2'W.
Bottom left: *Stele IV*, copper, 5'H × 4'W. Photograph: Mastorakos Studio.

JAMES T. RUSSELL

JAMES RUSSELL SCULPTURE ▨ 1930 LOMITA BOULEVARD ▨ LOMITA, CA 90717 ▨ TEL 310-326-0785
FAX 310-326-1470 ▨ E-MAIL JAMES@RUSSELLSCULPTURE.COM ▨ WWW.RUSSELLSCULPTURE.COM

216

Top: *Encounter in Flight II*, 1983, private residence, Pacific Palisades, CA, stainless steel, 9.5'H.
Bottom: *Timepiece*, 1985, Malibu, CA, stainless steel, 5.4'W.

TOM NEUGEBAUER

600 SAWKILL ROAD ▨ MILFORD, PA 18337 ▨ TEL 570-296-6901 ▨ FAX 570-296-9643
E-MAIL ARTISTS@PIKEONLINE.NET ▨ WWW.TOMNEUGEBAUER.COM

The Welcome, stainless steel, copper, brass and clay, 4' x 3' x 3'. Photograph: Bob Barrett. (See web link for outdoor installation view.)

KEVIN B. ROBB

KEVIN ROBB STUDIOS, LLC ■ 7001 WEST 35TH AVENUE ■ WHEAT RIDGE, CO 80033
TEL 303-431-4758 ■ FAX 303-425-8802 ■ E-MAIL 3D@KEVINROBB.COM ■ WWW.KEVINROBB.COM

218

Top left: *Dead Sea Series B*, 1999, cast bronze, 28" × 8" × 5". Photograph: John Bonath. Top right: *Falling Blocks*, 2000, fabricated bronze, 40" × 21" × 18". Photograph: John Bonath. Bottom right: *Swan Dance*, 2000, stainless steel, 94" × 36" × 29". Bottom left: *Toy Blocks II*, 1999, stainless steel, 121" × 40" × 32".

LUIS TORRUELLA

COND. TENERIFE APARTMENT 1201 ■ ASHFORD AVENUE 1507 ■ SAN JUAN, PR 00911 ■ TEL/FAX 787-722-8728 (STUDIO)
TEL 787-268-4977 (HOME) ■ E-MAIL LUISTORRUELLA@AOL.COM ■ WWW.LUISTORRUELLA.COM

Top: *Los Acróbatas*, 2002, aluminum, 10' × 12' × 6". Bottom: *Volumen Amarillo*, 1998, aluminum, 12' × 4' × 3'. Photographs: José Jimenez.

JEAN JUHLIN

JUHLIN SCULPTURE STUDIO ■ 764 NORTH 400 EAST ■ VALPARAISO, IN 46383-9721
TEL 219-464-0167 ■ E-MAIL JUHLINSTUDIO@MSN.COM ■ WWW.JUHLINSCULPTURE.COM

220

Top: *Spring Dreamer*, bronze. Bottom: *Cuzco Market Woman*, bronze.

RESOURCES

RESOURCES

THE CUSTOM DESIGN CENTER
A Project of GUILD.com

A commissioned work of art is a uniquely individual way to celebrate a family milestone, fill an unusual space or make everyday objects artful. This book gives you the essential tools to make that happen: photographs showing a range of products, media and art forms, and contact information so that you can connect directly with the artists whose work you want to own. For many *Artful Home* users, the path to custom-designed artworks is just this simple.

However, you may want to make use of another service available through the GUILD.com website. The GUILD Custom Design Center enables you to broadcast a description of your dream project to suitable artists via the Internet. Interested artists submit proposals free of charge, and you are under no financial obligation until you decide to proceed with a project.

GUILD.com

GUILD Custom Design

A handcrafted cradle for a first child? A portrait of a beloved grandparent? Whatever the project, the GUILD Custom Design Center can help make it a success.

www.guild.com/cdc

What kinds of projects pass through the Custom Design Center? Here are some examples:

- Lamps for a California bedroom

- Bar stools for a New York apartment

- Ceramic tiles for an Oklahoma kitchen

- Wall sconces for a California walkway and garden

- Indoor fountain for a Canadian home

Visit the GUILD Custom Design Center at www.guild.com/cdc, or call 877-344-8453 to discuss your idea with one of GUILD's Design Consultants. They can recommend candidates for a specific job, assess the qualifications of individual artists or help draft a letter of agreement.

ARTIST INFORMATION

ANAHATA ARTS
Garden Sculpture
Pages 3, 213

Eric David Laxman is an accomplished sculptor and furniture designer who works in a wide range of materials, including steel, bronze, stainless steel, wood, marble and granite. Laxman explores the abstract and the realistic by assembling stone fragments and welded metal into intricate compositions. He finds his inspiration from both Eastern and Western art traditions, and uses themes that express transformation, balance and movement. With Anahata Arts, Laxman has extended his unique sculptural sensibility to the realm of metal furniture and functional art. Laxman customizes his unique designs for particular tastes and environments by working closely with clients. Recent commissions include numerous decorative metal elements for Ashford and Simpson's Sugar Bar Restaurant, New York, NY and a bronze fountain for an estate in New Canaan, CT.

ATELIER BALL
Sculpture
Page 170

Hiram Ball strives to capture in bronze the human form and its range of emotions and movements, especially in daily life. "The human body is a marvel of engineering. My goal is to capture the inner feelings of the person I am sculpting, as well as the outer form, in a pleasing work of art — something that can be enjoyed in the home, office or garden." Current works are 10 to 18 inches in height, with pieces ranging from $750 to $4,000. Ball also does bas relief pieces. All pieces are available in larger sizes. Commissions and special projects are accepted.

CHAD AWALT
Sculpture
Page 171

Chad Awalt was inspired by his grandfather to pursue woodcarving from an early age. Awalt studied anatomy at the University of Colorado and has spent the last 20 years expanding his knowledge of classical design and traditional art. His abilities range from classical woodcarving to traditional oil painting, with a specialty for rendering the human figure. His flowing lines and light edges bring life and emotion to these spectacular life-size human forms. For over ten years, Awalt has been producing beautiful furniture and creating works of art that are sought after by clients and galleries all over the country. His work can be found in many corporate and private collections.

BORIS BALLY
Furniture
Pages 50-51, 134

Boris Bally's award-winning work is both witty and innovative, employing the use of a jeweler's skills on non-precious materials. The Urban Enamel series transforms selected recycled street signs into joyful objects. These distinctive pieces celebrate raw American street aesthetic in the form of useful objects for the home, and are collected for their bold imagery and weathered patina. Bally's work has received two Rhode Island Council on the Arts Fellowships in Design and a Pennsylvania Council on the Arts Fellowship. His work is featured in numerous international exhibitions and publications. Collections include the Victoria and Albert Museum, the Carnegie Museum of Art, the Brooklyn Museum, the Renwick Gallery and the Cooper Hewitt National Design Museum. Prices range from $70–$12,000. Special commissions are welcomed.

HARRIETT BELAG
Furniture
Pages 78-79

Harriett Belag works in terracotta, high-fired to stoneware for durability and strength. Each unique piece is painted in oils. The larger works are mounted on wheels for ease of movement. Belag's pieces function as sculptures, paintings and furniture at the same time. Although some of the work is available for immediate delivery, commissions are welcomed. Depending on the complexity of the work, most pieces can be shipped within 90 days of inception. The price range is from $1,500 to $8,000, plus shipping and handling from New York. Belag's work is found in many corporate and private collections, including the Shenley Corporation, Polygram Music Corporation, U.S. Industries and The White House collection of Senator Hillary Rodham Clinton.

BENNETT BEAN STUDIO
Floor Coverings
Pages 12, 121, 124

Bennett Bean has been known for his ceramic vessels for the last 20 years. Now he has turned his attention to a new medium. His rugs are the product of four years of exploration and interaction between the artist's sensibility, computerized design and the Tibetan rug-making tradition. The resulting series of rugs and carpets blend elements of contemporary imagery with ancient knotting techniques. Using the finest materials available, these rugs (tied at 100 knots per square inch) offer a luxuriant surface with excellent clarity of detail.

RON BENOIT
Furniture
Page 25

Ron Benoit creates furniture that bridges the gap between contemporary studio work and traditional American style. Employing design elements from classic styles, he relies on beautifully figured woods, clean lines and impeccable craftsmanship to achieve a timeless look that will enhance any environment. Benoit is self taught and has over 20 years of woodworking experience; his technique and style continue to evolve. Shop-sawn thick veneers, delicate inlays and sculpted hardwoods combine to create furniture that is as functional as it is beautiful. Most of his work is sold directly from his studio and may be seen there or at selected shows throughout the Rocky Mountain region. Shipping is available worldwide.

JONATHAN BENSON
Furniture
Page 38

Jonathan Benson's work has been influenced by many artistic sources over the past 26 years, including painting, sculpture and furniture design. Today, he often looks to the natural world for inspiration, particularly the geology, landscape and sky of the southwest United States, where he lives. After receiving his master's degree from the Rhode Island School of Design, Benson's style began to emerge. He combines turned wood with bent laminated panels of exotic veneers to create sturdy, elegant forms, which convey a unique sense of movement. He spends much time and effort searching for exceptional materials that add their own life and personality to his finished pieces. Benson has taught and lectured for many years. His work is in numerous private collections and is shown at galleries around the country.

SANDRA CHRISTINE Q. BERGÉR
Doors, Windows & Screens
Page 113

Internationally exhibited and published, award-winning glass designer Sandra Bergér creates exceptional custom glass art and limited editions for corporate, public and private clients. Precision-engineered, each glass sculpture or installation is effectively designed and executed. Experienced and professional, worldwide service, timely delivery. Recent projects: All Seasons, multicolored heirloom screen; glass art wall, Silicon Valley residence, CA; video magazine for PBS. Commissions: Concert Theatre, Minot, ND; Tanforan Business Center, South San Francisco, CA; White House, Washington, DC; Thermo King Corporation, Minneapolis, MN; public and private commissions. Publications: Designing Interiors textbook; Women in Design International, Facets magazine. Bergér's work has been featured in previous GUILD sourcebooks.

ARTIST INFORMATION

BOSTWICK DESIGNS
Furniture
Page 26

Terry Bostwick received his B.A. in painting and sculpture from San Francisco State University in 1974. He began making furniture in 1975, then moved to Portland, OR, in 1977, where he continues his career. His work has evolved from beautiful, yet unusual furniture of the 1970s, to a more conceptual exploration of form today. Bostwick's interest in Furniture History, and in particular the Art Nouveau, has led him to explore animal and plant forms, gesture and the suggestion of movement. His work ranges from small accessory pieces to large projects and has been placed in every room of the home or commercial space. With an element of irony, he does not always view furniture as purely an object of function. Yet, each piece is fully realized, both structurally and visually using traditional techniques.

SCOTT BRAUN
Furniture
Page 68

Scott Braun's designs begin with life: the tree, the vine, the human form. To create his work, trees are carefully selected and sawn apart in ways that complement specific designs. Individual parts are placed within each piece to support the design, both structurally and aesthetically. The finished piece exists like the tree itself, at peace and in harmony with its surroundings. Braun's one-of-a-kind pieces, custom commissions and limited-edition designs are elegant, timeless and original. "Scott Braun is separated from the rest by two things: his understanding of and ability to achieve graceful and sensual lines and his intimacy with the material. His attention to grain structure and its harmony within a piece is totally unparalleled." – Peter Fleming, Interior Designer, Boston, MA.

JOHN CLARK
Furniture
Page 24

John earned an M.F.A. in furniture design in 1986 from the Program in Artisanry at Boston University. He has been an artist in residence and the Wood Studio coordinator at Penland School in North Carolina over the past 17 years. He continues to maintain his own full-time studio in the same community. With strict concern for craftsmanship and an admiration for traditional furniture forms, Clark uses fine lumber and veneers to create pieces for individual clients and galleries. By working through a progression of ideas and drawings with his clients, his work reflects the desires and eccentricities of the owners. His furniture has been featured in *American Craft* magazine, *The New York Times* and *Fine Woodworking* magazine and can be found in many public and private collections.

WILLIAM D. BOSWORTH
Furniture
Page 47

Sculpture and master woodworker William D. Bosworth is the principal artist of W.D. Bosworth Woodworking and Sculpture. Since the age of 18, Bosworth has fulfilled his artful vision through sculpting and his self-taught woodworking talents. He has owned and operated woodworking businesses in and around his hometown of Newport, RI, and, for the past 12 years, in Beaufort, SC. Several years ago he extended his sculpting ambitions to full-time by founding a nonprofit corporation, the Environmental Art Association, which is now part of his woodworking business. Bosworth's newest endeavor includes the design and production of quality mahogany garden furniture inspired by his wife's love of gardening and the country way of life. This series includes a limited-edition line of furniture for the home.

BRUMDER FINE ART
Sculpture
Page 172

More than any other subject, the classic and timeless human figure has always fired the imagination of Polly Brumder. Working from life, she engages in the tactile quality of clay to begin translating the essence and vitality of the human form into bronze, an enduring material. She loves the way light plays on sculpture, as well as the power of form, its expansion and compression, movement and stillness. These qualities give her sculpture life and presence. Brumder has a background in painting, holding a B.F.A. from the University of Colorado. Her sculptural work has been exhibited with the National Sculpture Society and in Colorado.

JEREMY R. CLINE
Sculpture
Pages 204-205

The Birds of Paradise series illustrates Cline's interest in hand working molten glass to create an object of inherent movement and flexibility. Each piece, with its sensitive color palette and subtle undulating form, creates an ever-changing expression of the vessel as organic, suggesting both flower and bird. Cline's goal as a glassblower is to challenge himself to constantly improve his skills. As a result, his works explore a passion for an elusive perfection. In addition to this series, Cline also creates various other work by commission. Publications: *Contemporary Glass*, 2001; *Beautiful Things*, 2000.

LATCHEZAR BOYADJIEV
Sculpture
Page 206

Latchezar Boyadjiev is a graduate of the Academy of Applied Arts in Prague, Czech Republic, with training in sculptural glass. Latchezar currently resides in the San Francisco Bay area, where in 1988 he established his studio. By using cast-glass techniques, his work explores abstracting color, light and form. The monolithic castings range from one to six feet. The pieces can be integrated to create even larger architectural compositions. Boyadjiev's works are in museums and private collections in the United States and around the world. He exhibits in galleries and works on commissioned projects. Price range is $6,000 - $80,000.

CHRISTIANSEN-ARNER
Garden Sculpture
Page 214

The sculptures of Cherie Christiansen and Franz Arner bring together the natural elements of stone and water to create peaceful and healing environments for a variety of landscapes and interiors. These sculptures are often commissioned for indoor vestibules, entryways or courtyards. The stone water sculptures reflect both abstract sculptural shapes and the beauty and simplicity of the natural world, and they offer a retreat from the pressures of daily life. Commissions: numerous collections in northern California including Grace Family Vineyards, St. Helena, CA; Napier collection, Kentfiled, CA; Milstead sculpture collection, Orinda, CA; and Shozo Sato, Tea Master, Cleone, CA.

DAVID CODDAIRE
Furniture
Page 41

David Coddaire was born in Massachusetts, studied in Venice, Italy, and the Kansas City Art Institute. His sculpture, furniture, and printmaking has been shown throughout the U.S. and Europe in numerous exhibitions in addition to many private collections.

ARTIST INFORMATION

CHARIS CONGAIL
Sculpture
Page 173

Studying and portraying the many complicated features and expressions of the human face brings Charis Congail a great deal of enjoyment. Expression is paramount in her work, and her goal is for every piece to contain a strong emotional element. In addition to portraiture, Congail is currently creating a new series of original and limited-edition figurative works. Congail graduated magna cum laude from the University of Wisconsin with a B.F.A. in sculpture and a B.S. in comparative religious studies. She is a member of the National Sculpture Society and Wisconsin Painters and Sculptors. She accepts commissioned works for private and public settings. Her sculptures can be completed in a variety of materials, including gypsum and bronze.

GWENN CONNOLLY
Sculpture
Pages 169, 176-177

The emotion of Gwenn Connolly's sculpture transcends the human form, speaking to the deep universal human truths of hope, strength and courage. Indoors or outdoors, in a public place or a private corner, her works resonate with the viewer's spirit. They are assertive in their movement. They are affirmative. They are celebratory, and they invite and encourage the viewer to stop, to look and to feel the affirmation and joy of life. Connolly's sculpture is suitable for a range of public and private environments, including residences, gardens, health care facilities, corporate settings and resorts.

STEPHAN J. COX
Sculpture
Pages 198-199

Stephan J. Cox has been compelled to make things since childhood. In 1979 he was working on printmaking at the University of Wisconsin – River Falls. The glass shop was next door and he found himself drawn to that hot, high-energy environment. The tricky molten material took over his life, and since that time he has worked exclusively with glass, continually studying the interplay between form, color, texture and light. "I imagine a fantastical object and work in glass to create it. The journey from idea to object is always fascinating." Cox recently completed a major piece on commission for the Wild Rice restaurant in Bayfield, WI, and is represented in numerous public and private collections, including the Corning Museum of Glass, Corning, NY.

SUZANNE CRANE
Objects
Page 146

Suzanne Crane's fine functional stoneware is inspired by the arts and crafts movement, nineteenth-century natural history book illustrations and an appreciation of the fractal geometry found in nature. Each piece is made by hand on a potter's wheel using real botanical specimens as templates for glazing. Each piece is, therefore, entirely unique. Commissions are welcome for dinnerware, sink basins and tile work for kitchens, baths, fireplaces or floors. Decorative stoneware baskets, platters, large bowls, funeral urns, vases, candlesticks and lamps are also available. Suzanne Crane shows her work in her Virginia studio/gallery, at quality fine arts and crafts fairs across the nation, at select fine craft galleries and on GUILD.com.

ROBERT DANE
Objects
Pages 140-141

Robert Dane is an internationally known sculptor and glassblower. He has worked in his studio in Heath, Massachusetts, for over 20 years. He and his wife, Jayne, also co-own the Dane Gallery of Nantucket Island. "The beauty of nature continues to inspire me and inform my work. We are often too absorbed by the day-to-day details of our own small existence to visualize and recognize the grand scheme that is transpiring around us. My aim is to celebrate the beauty of the progression of life as it unfolds and reveals itself." Collections include: the Philadelphia Museum of Art, the American Craft Museum and the Corning Museum of Glass. Dane also produces a line of functional glassware, inspired by the Venetian tradition. His one-of-a-kind *Tutti Frutti Goblets* lend a sense of playfulness and elegance to any table.

DANI
Sculpture
Page 187

Dani is well known for her exquisite, highly detailed bronze sculptures. She rarely uses models but creates an entire piece in her mind before executing her work, using anatomy books as reference for measurements. This creative process takes about three months, then she begins her foundry work. With 30 years experience and many one-woman shows and awards, Dani holds a membership in the California Arts Club, the Academy of Fine Arts Foundation, the San Diego Art Institute, the Catharine Lorillard Wolfe Art Club, the Hudson Valley Art Club and the American Artists Professional League. In 1984 Dani was inducted into the Orange Coast College Hall of Fame. Publications include: *South West Art* magazine; "Dream Woman Exists," *Los Angeles Times*; *Artists in the 1990s*; *Outstanding People of the 20th Century*; and *Who's Who in American Art.*

PETER F. DELLERT
Furniture
Page 32

Peter Dellert creates architecturally and biomorphically inspired, meticulously crafted mixed-media wall-mounted cabinets. Materials and techniques include polychromed wood, patinated copper panels and hardware, curved laminations, carving, veneers, collage, gold leaf and integral lighting using recycled glass lenses. Closed, they are formal, crisp, and monumental; opened, they reveal levels of detail both classical and whimsical, beckoning the viewer to further investigate meaning and intent. Recent shows include: Sculpture Invitational, 2002, Norman Rockwell Museum, Stockbridge, MA; Philadelphia Furniture Show, 2002; Gallery at the Clown, 2001, Portland, ME; Lucky Street Gallery, 2002 and 2001, Key West, FL; McKeen Gallery, 1999, Boston, MA.

LOUIS DeMARTINO
Architectural Details
Page 98

Louis DeMartino sculpts original architectural elements, such as doors, gates, windows, fountains and fences, in bronze and stainless steel. His studio, foundry and staff of artisans are located in a mountain valley above Palm Springs, CA. He has lived in New York, Italy and the South Pacific, but works on commissions all over the world. As a sculptor, he prefers to highlight architectural elements without distracting from the overall design. He seeks to interpret the locations and to take into account the client and architect's visions. Commissions: City of San Francisco, CA; Pacific Telephone; City of Duluth, MN; City of La Quinta, CA; City of Ohara, Japan; City of Los Angeles, CA; United States Olympic Swimming, Colorado Springs, CO; Malcolm Forbes, New York, NY; Lladro, Spain; Frank Sinatra, Palm Springs, CA.

DEMETRIOS & EAMES
Sculpture
Page 194

Llisa Demetrios creates sculpture for contemplative retreats set in homes and private gardens. Working in bronze to create abstract forms, she shapes sculpture that is universally approachable but has an individual impact. Lucia Eames designs large and small tables, benches, gates, screens and sculptures in bronze, steel and aluminum. The pieces are used indoors and outdoors. The positive/negative patterns provide modulated light and cast rich shadows. The work of Demetrios and Eames is featured in previous GUILD sourcebooks.

ARTIST INFORMATION

HAMILTON S. DIXON
Furniture
Page 70

Hamilton Dixon has been sculpting steel as an art form for more than 20 years. He has developed a distinctive style that combines striking forcefulness and fluidity in perfect balance. Dixon chose metal as a medium because of its weight, texture, and most of all, permanence. To manipulate steel, he uses a gas forge, anvil and power hammer. Finished artwork includes large freestanding sculpture as well as gates, railings, weathervanes and interior furnishings such as beds, mirrors and tables. Works can be found in museum, public and private collections throughout the United States.

"If steel were alive, how would it grow . . . as if given birth by his anvil."

—Ron Beam, poet

MICHAEL DOERR
Furniture
Pages 21, 62

Michael Doerr began his career as a wooden shipwright; his love of workmanship has evolved into furniture making with a focus on comfort, function and an eye for clarity of line. Doerr is nationally known for his sculptural chairs, which are represented in the Parson School of Design/Smithsonian Institute lecture series, "Contemporary American Crafts." Since the founding of Doerr Woodworking in 1989, a national and international clientele has developed. All furniture is handmade by commission; collaboration between the artisan and client creates the opportunity to select the sizes, wood type and grain that will best enhance a quality piece of furniture. Doerr's shop is a place where the soul of the tree meets the spirit of the craftsman.

EARTH FIRE DESIGNS
Architectural Details
Pages 16, 95

Michael King combines clay, metal and glass to create works of art that uplift and inspire the romantic in all of us. He specializes in custom fireplace surrounds, sculpted murals and fine art wall-mounted sculptures. He received a B.F.A. in sculpture from the University of Wisconsin-Milwaukee in 1979. His work has been collected nationally and featured on the Discovery Channel. Studio services range from concept drawings to installation. Prices, samples and a portfolio are available on request.

DAVID EBNER
Furniture
Page 64

David Ebner is an artist/craftsman who works in four modes: classical impressions of furniture, turned objects, sculptural furniture and sculpture. "I approach my art intuitively as well as intellectually, drawing inspiration wherever I find it. I've explored a variety of directions and themes over the years, but each piece is treated as an art object with concern for my material and honesty to its inherent qualities. For me, one's creative ability is demonstrated in the diversity of the pieces and what one learns from change." Working with the artisans at Mussi ArtWorks Foundry in California, Ebner has recently translated some of his classic wood pieces into bronze. Collections include: National Collection of Fine Art, Smithsonian Institution, Washington, DC; American Craft Museum, New York, NY; and the Museum of Fine Arts, Boston, MA.

FAUNA COLLECTION
Furniture
Page 75

Fauna Collection's five elegant chairs and table are the creation of sculptor-designer Ray Lewis, who carved the originals in wood. Sand-cast in aluminum alloys and hand-polished to a silvery finish, the signed and numbered chairs are upholstered in black leather; each bears an animal motif: dolphin, eagle, impala, rabbit and horse. Designed for fantasy and function, the Fauna chairs are both comfortable and dazzling. They have been featured in galleries across the country and exhibited in Atlanta's International Museum of Art and Design, an affiliate of the Smithsonian Institute. Eight *Eagle Chairs* were featured in Buena Vista's motion picture Aspen Extreme. The *Eagle Chair* also garnered the Niche Award for Sculpture. (Not pictured in this publication are the *Horse Chair* and table.)

CAROLE A. FEUERMAN
Sculpture
Page 186

For over 30 years, Carole Feuerman has created and exhibited sculptures worldwide. Her newest works are figurative bronzes. She is the recipient of the Amelia Peabody Award and the Lorenzo De Medici Prize. Her sculptures are in the permanent museum collections of the Bass Museum of Art, Miami, FL; Lowe Art Museum, Coral Galbes, FL; Tampa Museum of Art, FL; Southern Alleghenies Museum of Art, PA; and Queensborough Community College, Bayside, NY. Other collections include: President Clinton, Senator Hillary Rodham Clinton, Dr. Henry Kissinger, the Caldic Collection, the Weisman Foundation, the Absolut Art Collection and the Malcolm Forbes Collection. Hudson Hills recently published her coffee table book, *Carole Feuerman: Sculptor*, which features photos by David Finn.

BILL AND SANDY FIFIELD
Furniture
Page 60

Bill and Sandy Fifield have worked together for over 35 years, collaborating on separate projects in wood and stained glass. Bill Fifield is a self-taught wood artist who has been greatly influenced by both classical carving techniques and folk art from all over the world. His work has included doors, desks, tables, chairs, cabinets, mantels, pillars, lecterns, corbels and chests, with or without glass. Sandy Fifield's work includes all of the new windows for St. Mary's Anglican Catholic Church in Denver, CO, as well as panels and lamps for private homes all over the United States. Over 95% of their work is by commission; they particularly love to work on new and challenging projects incorporating wood and glass.

MARY FISCHER
Sculpture
Page 197

Mary Fischer's interest in things architectural is expressed in her work with clay. Sculptural pieces are made from slabs and extruded pieces of clay. Occasionally nails and bristles from brushes are incorporated. The process of building sculpture is often akin to playing with legos or tinker toys: sometimes the finished pieces are made up of parts that can be rearranged, so the process of playing with clay continues. Exhibitions: All School Exhibition, Southwest School of Art and Craft, San Antonio, TX; invited artist and panelist, 16th Annual San Angelo Ceramic Symposium, San Angelo Museum of Fine Arts, San Angelo, TX; *From the Ground Up: Contemporary Clay in Texas*, Austin Museum of Art-Laguna Gloria, Austin, TX; Monarch National Ceramic Competition, Kennedy-Douglas Center for the Arts, Florence, AL.

BARBARA FLETCHER
Lighting
Page 86

Barbara Fletcher's humor and excellent use of color, texture and delight in the animal and natural world shine through in her works of art. She enjoys the challenge of unique commissions, including a recent life-size sculpture of a woman diving into water. Other interesting private commissions include a wall-mounted dimensional rock and fish aquarium, and planet mobiles. The durability of the material she uses makes her work appropriate for public collections; her experience with this setting includes many hospitals and restaurants. Fletcher's work can be seen in the book, *Paper Illuminated*, which features her illuminated paper sculptures; *A Complete Guide to Paper Casting*, by Arnold Grummer; and *Paper Making for the First Time*, by Rhonda Rainey, which showcases her cast paper work. Prices range from $150-$3,000.

ARTIST INFORMATION

STEVE FONTANINI
Architectural Details
Page 99

The confluence of the Snake and Hoback rivers is where Steve Fontanini and company produce metalwork of all kinds. Stair railings, gates and chandeliers are made to your design, or they will be happy to design to fit your needs. Projects are built by forging hot metal and joining the pieces with traditional methods such as rivets, collars and mortise-and-tenon joints. Fontanini's work is found throughout the United States. Awards include the Silver award for forged interior railings, 2002, National Ornamental and Miscellaneous Metals Association (NOMMA).

GERRY LEISTIKOW DESIGN
Furniture
Page 66

Gerry Leistikow sculpts in wood and other materials, creating furniture and pieces of unusual and intriguing form that he conceives as utilitarian sculpture. Working in wood, metal, plastics and various other materials, Leistikow brings a long history of design, from handcrafted to mass-produced, to the design and construction of one-of-a-kind and limited-production works, including seating, dining, storage and accessories. Leistikow designs, crafts and creates original, contemporary art for all environments and is available to design for industry and manufacture. His current work is focused on a line of stunning and unusual upholstered seating.

GLENN GILMORE
Architectural Details
Pages 92-93, 151

Award-winning artist Glenn Gilmore designs and executes site-specific architectural metalwork for residential interiors and exteriors throughout the United States. Gilmore works in ferrous and non-ferrous metals and has the ability to bring great life to the material as he creates visually pleasing forged metalwork. With 29 years of experience, he designs and creates one-of-a-kind pieces with care and diligence. Collaborating with interior designers, architects and individual clients, he will design the appropriate commission to enhance your specific environment. Gilmore is well known for his award-winning fireplace screens and hearth tools, yet he also creates beautiful gates, light fixtures, grills and decorative fence work.

DANIEL B. GLANZ
Sculpture
Page 178

Through his bronze sculpture, Glanz captures a timeless intimacy for the viewer. Both his figurative and wildlife work share a powerful yet elegant quality, drawn from his classical approach to sculpture. Using his strong sense of balance, design and texture, he brings out the subtlest aspects of all his subjects. An award-winning sculptor, Glanz began his career in illustration and fine art photography with The Smithsonian Institute. His sculptures, which are created in his studio in Colorado, range in size from table top to monumental. His editions and commissions grace many private collections and public art programs.

JENNA GOLDBERG
Furniture
Page 36

Jenna Goldberg received her M.F.A. in furniture design from the Rhode Island School of Design and a B.F.A. in illustration from The University of the Arts. She has taught at several professional schools and has been a visiting lecturer at the Renwick Gallery in Washington, DC. Her work can be seen at various galleries, including Clark Gallery in Lincoln, MA, and Pritam and Eames Gallery in East Hampton, NY. She was the recipient of the 2000 North Carolina Arts Council Award and is in the permanent collection of the Mint Museum of Craft and Design. Her work includes cabinets, tables and wall-hung vanities, which borrow elements from American furniture, as well as decorative designs from other cultures. The rhythm of overlapping colors and patterns integrate with compartments and openings, constructing a sense of history and familiarity within.

BILL GOSSMAN
Objects
Page 147

The universal powers of earth, water, air and fire are embodied in the intimate, intense wood-fired pottery of Bill Gossman. This man's pottery is an evolution of time, travel and talent, a flow of energy that forms nature's elements into the artist's most personal, exquisite expression. The evolution of Gossman's work is a blend of inspiration from Africa, Europe and North America. The elements of each country, experience and thought are made manifest in each new piece. From Swaziland, Africa: the freedom of free-flowing, functional pottery. From Denmark: the strength, purity and discipline of demanding, straight-line pottery. From the United States: diverse style and statements from rich natural resources and a multicultural community. The vortex of Gossman's art reflects a culmination of his life. The result is a mature, complex body of work.

GRACE POMERLEAU FURNITURE STUDIO
Furniture
Page 59

Grace Pomerleau and her associates create a line of exquisitely hand-carved and intricately detailed luxury beds in their Vermont studio. Pomerleau considers her sculpted beds to be "usable art," emphasizing her belief that the bed itself should be the focus of the bedroom. Grace Pomerleau Furniture Studio's designs fuse historical perspective and old world craftsmanship with state-of-the-art techniques to ensure that each piece will be enjoyed for generations.

CAROL GREEN
Objects
Pages 136, 168

It takes insight, confidence and the mastery of materials to tackle forms imbued with historical, cultural and spiritual meaning and to achieve fresh, vibrant results. Carol Green accomplishes exactly that in creating serene, Zen-like sculptural vessels, the most poignant examples of which are her *Ikebana* patinated bronze works. Green's vessels underscore the value of a solid education in the arts: a B.F.A. from the Art Institute of Chicago, an M.F.A. in metalsmithing from Cranbrook Academy and an M.A. in popular culture from Bowling Green State University. She also has 30 years experience in the studio and an artist's intent to honor her subjects with grace and skill. In Green's experienced hands, earthy, organic materials transcend the ordinary to become exquisite examples of archetypal elegance. Her successful melding of clay and metal is appreciated by collectors worldwide.

GREGG LIPTON FURNITURE
Furniture
Pages 69, 88

Gregg Lipton's primary aim is to bring his unique sense of beauty and utility into people's homes and places of business. Simplicity in form, edge, line, shadow and proportion are the elements that he concerns himself with while designing. As in nature, Lipton believes that equilibrium in design is achieved when nothing can be added, nothing taken away. Selected exhibitions, collections and publications include: New Britain Museum of American Art, New Britain, CT; Portland Museum of Art Biennial 2001; Smithsonian Craft Show; Philadelphia Museum of Art Craft Show; Oprah Winfrey Productions, Chicago, IL; Gramercy Tavern, New York, NY; Eleven Madison Park, New York, NY; Tabla, New York, NY; *Object Lessons*, 2001; *The Custom Furniture Sourcebook*, 2001.

LYDIA GREY
Objects
Page 150

"With clay and my hands, I work to put the deepest feelings of my heart into a form that can be seen, held and felt." Using stories told by friends, myths, folktales and personal experiences, Lydia Grey makes story pots. She begins by throwing porcelain clay on the wheel. She pushes the walls of the pot in and out with her fingers to make the figures. Details such as faces, hands and feet are added, shaped by hand. When dry, pots are smoothed and layered with terra sigillata. Each layer is burnished to make a soft, touchable surface. Finally, the pots are smoke-fired with sawdust and leaves in an outdoor pit, where the smoke, fire, clay and leaves interact to create a range of effects.

DIANA HARRISON
Lighting
Pages 13, 83, 87, 202

Diana Harrison's sculpture has always been about scale and natural form, and now with her lamps, she has added the element of light. The translucency of the paper lends itself very well to the flower forms … they are the garden that you don't have to water. The forms are made from Japanese handmade paper made from Kozo, a processed mulberry bark. She adds pigments and stiffener to the paper and places it into molds, from which she makes her sculptures. It then dries in shapes, which she places around the lamp. The shapes of her pieces stay the same but the colors can change. New designs can be made for an added fee.

CHERYL HAZAN
Furniture
Page 58

Anandamali introduces its new line of contemporary furniture and accessories, the Fusion Collection, Art as Furniture, designed and created by Cheryl Hazan and Marti Sagar. The collection includes functional and beautiful dining tables, nightstands, end tables, consoles and mirrors, all of which are unique. The signed pieces combine hardwoods such as cherry, walnut, pear and teak with inlaid glass mosaics. Custom work is their trademark and installations include bathrooms, backsplashes, countertops, mosaic carpets and art murals. Anandamali was named among the "Home Team" of designers by *New York* magazine: "Behind New York's most spectacular interiors are special effects dream teams, whose names are carefully guarded in the Rolodexes of the city's top architects and interior designers."

SCOTT GROVE
Furniture
Page 40

Scott Grove creates contemporary, classic art furniture with a harmonious blend of uniquely carved textures, rich finishes and woods with radiant figured grains. Each of Grove's works has a unique tactile quality that begs to be touched. A sense of wonder will be raised by the sophisticated and elegant style, which is accented with a touch of whimsy. Each piece is handcrafted, one at a time. Custom orders can easily be produced. For over 25 years, Grove has been working directly with designers, architects and private collectors to keep their interests in focus. He offers many design options that can be matched to suit your specific requirements. Commercial and residential projects are welcome. Represented nationwide, Scott Grove has won numerous awards and has been featured on Home & Garden's television channel, HGTV.

STEVE HASSLOCK
Architectural Details
Pages 91, 94

Steve Hasslock's primary medium is clay. Over the last 30 years he has worked with various types of clay, methods and glazing. "Sculptural work carries the passion of my heart. The sensuousness of clay in its wet state is the wellspring from which the joy of creation emanates." The challenges of size, location, budget and color add to the creative process. Hasslock has completed a variety of private and public commissions. His studio is large enough to accommodate just about any size project. Hasslock Studios has also featured a line of majolica for the last 12 years, including dinnerware, painted tiles for kitchen and bath, swimming pools and fountains.

KAREN HEYL
Garden Sculpture
Page 211

Using Indiana limestone, Karen Heyl carves stylized figurative, natural and organic forms to enhance a garden setting. Her relief carvings are custom commissions and reflect ideas shared between client and artist. Works include monolithic shapes carved in the round, as well as one-sided flat stones that can be mounted on a base, pedestal or wall. Heyl creates aesthetic sophistication with simplified, sensual forms suitable for the home garden, memorial garden, patio, courtyard or entryway. Heyl has been creating stone sculpture for 20 years. She has large-scale relief carvings throughout the U.S. in parks, corporate buildings, churches, hospitals, convention centers and universities. Her work has been featured in previous GUILD sourcebooks.

RAIN HARRIS
Sculpture
Page 196

Rain Harris received her B.A. from the Rhode Island School of Design. She is currently a resident artist at the Clay Studio in Philadelphia, PA. Her work has been exhibited in group shows at the U.S. Chamber of Commerce, Washington, DC; Holter Museum of Art, Helena, MT; the Philadelphia Art Alliance, PA; the Craft Alliance, St. Louis, MO; and the Holler Gallery, State College, PA, among others. Solo shows include Objects of Desire, Louisville, KY; the Philadelphia International Airport; and Nexus. Awards include the Leeway Grant for Achievement, an American Craft Council Emerging Artist grant and an Independence Foundation fellowship. Her work has been reviewed in various publications and was recently purchased by the San Angelo Museum of Fine Arts. Her work is also found in national and international private collections.

HOWARD HATCH
Furniture
Page 46

Howard Hatch has been designing custom residential, institutional and liturgical furniture at his studio in Conway, New Hampshire, since 1976. An avid pool player, Hatch was pleased to design a pool table for a private collector. Inspiration for the mahogany table shown in this publication comes from the ocean, with hand-carved shell fluting on the legs, an inlaid wave made from holly and sights of inlaid mother-of-pearl along the top edge. Chairs are designed with a full-scale mockup made for the client to test before the final piece is constructed. Hatch believes that a good chair is sculptural, comfortable and evocative of the human body. Notable commissions include churches, libraries, the Governor's Council Chamber and the Federal District Court Judges' Chambers in Concord, NH.

BILL HOPEN
Sculpture
Page 185

Bill Hopen's sculptures are individually cast, finished, patinaed and mounted by hand. His major works are in museums and public gardens throughout the U.S. and in corporate and private collections. Shown in this publication are examples of his work in the price range of $400 to $2,000. Works are available shipped directly from the artist, through galleries or through your designer. "Hopen's small bronzes make potent accent pieces for any interior design, but they are more than decorative, they are art; they impact the heart, thrill the body and mind of those who see and hold them."—Judy Politi, Stavroff Design Associates

ARTIST INFORMATION

DAVID L. HOSTETLER
Sculpture
Page 180

David L. Hostetler draws his inspiration from mythological, folk and pop culture sources. He has become a wholly original creator of female figures carved directly from American hardwoods and exotic woods such as ziricote, zebrawood and purpleheart. Hostetler's bronzes are cast from the woodcarvings, thereby developing the imagery with painterly patinas, brilliant coloring and polished surfaces. *David L. Hostetler: The Carver*, published by Ohio University Press, chronicles his life and work. Recent large-scale commissions are at Trump International Hotel and Tower, New York, NY; and Grounds for Sculpture, Hamilton, NJ. His sculptures can also be found in over 25 museums. "I love to carve wood. I am passionate about the tactile quality of wood, its color and its connection to humanity. Wood is a living material, never static."

JENNIFER JACOBY
Doors, Windows & Screens
Page 120

Jennifer Jacoby's unique folding screens are constructed from steel, art glass and high-fire paints. Her work is inspired by contemporary design elements and traditional practices such as stained glass and painting on glass. This body of work deals with the duality between nature and art through form, line, light and color. Jacoby draws on skills that were developed while completing apprenticeships in Sienna, Italy, and London, England, prior to earning a bachelor of fine arts degree.

EILEEN JAGER
Furniture
Pages 53, 246

The dance between glass and light is endlessly fascinating for Eileen Jager. It's been her passion since a magical moment at Chartres Cathedral when the power of light and color transformed her. Eileen is inspired by beauty, nature and the balance of form and function. Each piece she creates is a journey revealed through vision, trust and perseverance. Her glass mosaic furniture and "aquaturo"—or table-fountains—are functional, multidimensional and luscious. They're a sensory delight to see, hear, touch and experience. Iridescent glass shimmers while water gently flows. Jager is moved by the power of art to enhance our lives. She welcomes commissions and has recently completed a project inspired by Michelangelo's *Piazza del Campidoglio* in Rome. Prices range from $2,500 to $18,000.

SUZANNE JANSE-VREELING
Furniture
Page 72

Suzanne Janse-Vreeling is an artistic welder and designer of custom metalwork. All of her works are one of a kind and include railings, chairs, beds, pot racks, benches, gates, arbors and fireplace doors. She also incorporates upholstery and mosaic into some pieces, such as interior furniture or tables with mosaic tops and metal bases. Janse-Vreeling is inspired by the fluid lines and subtle forms found in nature, hammering them out in mild steel. Since 1989 she has been creating works primarily for private clients. She has been featured in *MPLS.ST.PAUL* magazine and recently finished a large commission for a local sushi restaurant.

DALE JENSSEN
Architectural Details
Page 102

Specializing in custom lighting, Dale Jenssen creates individual architectural elements and complete interiors that are infused with sensuality and humor. Impeccable craftsmanship and integrated design are the hallmarks of her work. For over 20 years, Jenssen has been creating works using wood, metals, plastics and recycled items in unique and refreshing combinations. Numerous private, public and commercial clients have commissioned her sconces, mirror frames, lamps and sculptures. The challenges inherent in custom work stimulate new ideas and engender personal and artistic growth for Jenssen. She takes great joy in collaborating with individual clients and with fellow design professionals to create works that inspire and are fun to live with.

JOHN LEWIS GLASS STUDIO
Furniture
Page 76

John Lewis has owned and operated a glass production studio in Oakland, California, for the past 32 years. Lewis designs and produces cast-glass sculpture, tables, vessels and site-specific architectural projects. He has completed numerous commissions for private and corporate clients and is represented internationally by galleries. His primary sources of inspiration have been the exploration of casting methods and glass in the molten state. Commissions include: Morgan Stanley, New York, NY; Singapore Fountain Project, Han Sai Por; Oklahoma City Memorial, OK; San Francisco International Airport, CA; San Jose Veterans Memorial, CA. His work is found in the American Craft Museum, New York, NY; Darmstadt Museum, Switzerland; Metropolitan Museum of Art, New York, NY; and the Boston Museum of Fine Arts, MA.

PATRICK JOHNSON
Objects
Page 153

Patrick Johnson learned about art at an early age from his father, Max Johnson. Later he worked for his father's advertising agency and earned a B.F.A. in painting and art history. In 1988 he began working in clay, which has become his primary medium. The clay is worked using several hand-building techniques, such as press mold, slab, carved, impressed and pinched construction, depending on the desired result. Different clay bodies – stonewares and porcelain – can be pressed or laminated together to create texture and movement. The surfaces are finished with layers of slips and glaze wash, then fired in reduction. "As a wilderness traveler, I am inspired by the natural beauty of the world and the loved ones who often accompany me there."

JORDAN
Architectural Details
Page 100

Imagine copper, bronze, stainless and mild steels and even titanium heating in the forge to a glowing orange, moving it to the anvil and striking the malleable metal with a hammer to change its shape from something plain and simple to something unique and beautiful. After two decades of practice, an artistic eye and a desire for perfection, Jordan's work has reached homes and corporate offices across America. Whatever the style or design by the architect, designer, client or the artist himself, each piece is given the attention it needs to become a work of art.

JEAN JUHLIN
Garden Sculpture
Page 220

Jean Juhlin was born and raised in Chicago, where she attended the Art Institute. She has been creating sculpture in bronze for the past 40 years. Her commissioned sculptures can be found around the world in the corporate environment, schools, libraries, hospitals and places of worship, as well as private home and garden environments. Her representational sculpture is generally life-sized and larger. Juhlin is presently working on two heroic-sized Mexican Indian women for a fountain installation commissioned by Rancho La Puerta, a health spa in Tecate, Mexico.

ARTIST INFORMATION

MARY DENNIS KANNAPELL
Sculpture
Page 189

Mary Dennis Kannapell is a multi-disciplinary artist and designer. She studied sculpture and theater at Edgecliff College and continued her studies in sculpture, illustration and graphic design at Cincinnati Art Academy, Xavier University, Parsons School of Design and the American Museum of Natural History. She has worked as a designer, craftsman, muralist and art director for such clients as Henson Associates, Quaker Oats, Bette Midler, the Louisville Zoo, Stage One, Actors Theatre and many others. Her work has won numerous awards and has been exhibited both internationally and regionally. She continues her work in a broad range of media including clay, fiber and glass.

RAIN KIERNAN
Garden Sculpture
Page 210

Rain Kiernan creates sculpture in marble, bronze, stainless steel and alternative media, including fiberglass and cement. Her abstracts include both large-scale outdoor works and smaller interior sculpture. Kiernan's forms are both free-form and derivative and are characterized by her unique style, which features powerful but sensuous curves, relieved by supporting planes. The artist has won several awards of merit for sculpture and is represented in various U.S. galleries. Kiernan, who has been showing her sculpture professionally since 1990, creates work for public parks, commercial property and private residences. Commissions: Bristol Community College, Fall River, MA; Waveny Public Park, New Canaan, CT; private homes and businesses in New York City, Atlanta, Palm Beach, Greenwich, CT, and Southampton, NY.

LAVEZZO DESIGNS
Furniture
Page 77

Janel and Robert Lavezzo have been in business since 1996, providing high-end custom furniture, railings and other home items to their San Francisco Bay Area clients. They have been featured in the San Francisco Chronicle and Interiors magazine and have won awards for their pieces. Through Robert's 23 years of experience in metal fabrication and Janel's intuitive, creative design sense, they produce beautiful and interesting pieces of functional art. "We work with the natural qualities of the materials so that what you see is a true reflection of their inherent beauty. We find that our pieces interact with the surrounding environment and convey a sense of serenity and balance." All of Lavezzo Designs' pieces are signed, dated and numbered by the artists.

BJ KATZ
Architectural Details
Pages 104-105

Glass artist BJ Katz developed a technique combining glass casting, draping and painting. Her signature artwork, torsos, metaphorically explore the uniqueness of human existence, drawing attention to the juxtaposition of the inner emotional and psychological world and appearance or image. Commissions include: Water wall, Desert Ridge Mall; Chapel wall, TX Children's Hospital; lobby sculpture, Phelps Dodge Hdqtrs; signage, Phoenix Children's Hospital; Torso, Scottsdale Healthcare Foundation. Collections include: the International Cat Museum, Amsterdam; Yellow-eyed Penguin Conservatory, Dunedin, New Zealand; and the American Express Corp. Katz is a featured artist in the television documentary, Women Artisans, on "Modern Masters," HGTV, 2002. Awards include the Regional Craftsmanship Award for Art in Architecture, SW Region, Construction Specification Institute, 2000.

KINOE KOMODA DESIGNS
Furniture
Page 39

Kinoe Komoda Designs specializes in furniture that combines the vibrancy and spirit of American studio furniture with the mystery and simplicity of Asian aesthetics and design. This hybridization of West and East presents itself in both a quiet and bold presence. The Kinoe Komoda design portfolio is very versatile and can be customized in a variety of ways – a single design can be applied to a bench, coffee table or hall table, for instance. Choices of wood and color make each piece unique and personal.

CLIFF LEE
Sculpture
Page 207

"I want my work to express a sensitive and honest use of the material and technique. I hope it will embody the eternal quality of aesthetic joy." Permanent collections: The White House Collection of American Craft, Washington, DC; Renwick Gallery, Washington, DC; National Museum of American Art, Washington, DC; Smithsonian Institution, Washington, DC; Mint Museum of Craft and Design, Charlotte, NC; Columbia Museum of Art, Columbia, SC; American Craft Museum, New York, NY.

TOM KENDALL
Objects
Page 152

Tom Kendall has been a studio potter, sculptor and educator for over 30 years. Throughout his career he has held fast to his conviction that even the smallest utilitarian vessels require devoted attention to detail. His porcelains, as well as his mixed-media and metal sculptures, are in numerous public and private collections. Tom's porcelains explore the relationship between strong vessel forms and landscape-inspired surfaces. Unexpected random patterns in nature have become a dominant theme. By layering and blending glazes on wet clay, he captures the feeling of light and shadow in the heart of a deep woodland with a painterly flair. Forms are chosen to enhance the qualities of the surfaces. The bodies of the vessels resemble smooth beach stones, while the spouts and handles are reminiscent of leaves.

ERIN LAREAU
Objects
Page 167

"I began with a glass slipper . . . working in the magical medium of Pavé Crystal. By individually placing thousands of crystal gems, I pave objects with luminous jewels, transforming them into icons. Dazzling objets de fantasie evoke fantasy, mirage and kinetic light. They shimmer and change color as you walk by." Seen at the Academy Awards, Tiffany's and various art museums, Erin Lareau's objets de fantasie have been presented to the President of Turkmenistan, Oprah, Elton John, Bette Midler and other celebrities. They have been featured on "Sex in the City," "Friends," and "Will & Grace," to name a few. Lareau's work has been featured at the Orange County Museum of Art, COPIA, the Museum of Television and Radio, and the Peterson Museum. Functional art, home accessories, fine art and fun jewelry from $25 to $15,000.

ALAN LeQUIRE
Sculpture
Page 188

Alan LeQuire is a figurative sculptor, well known in his native Southeast for his public commissions and sensitive portraiture. LeQuire works in a variety of sculptural materials, including wood, stone and cast bronze. He has completed a number of architectural, collaborative and site-specific projects since he began accepting commissions in 1981. Recent projects: Musica, monumental figurative sculpture, Nashville, TN; portrait group, three life-size bronze figures, Columbia/Hospital Corporation of America, Nashville, TN and Hudson, FL; Nashville Public Library doors, 24 relief panels in bronze, TN; Jack Daniels, life-size bronze portrait, Jack Daniels Distillery, Lynchburg, TN and Louisville, KY; Teacher and Student, life-size bronze, Montgomery Bell Academy, Nashville, TN.

ARTIST INFORMATION

MARK LEVIN
Furniture
Page 63

Mark Levin uses solid wood in his work for its sculptural malleability and creative viability. The aesthetic linchpins that drive Levin's creations are sensuality and delicacy. His work has a mellifluous dynamic similar to that of a Beethoven passage, weaving melodic filigree out of molten steel. Work is executed on a commission basis for both residential and commercial clients. Exhibitions and awards: Niche Award, 2002; First Place, National Custom Woodworking Business Design Portfolio; First Place, Artisans of the New Forest National Exhibition. Recent publications: *The Custom Furniture Source Book, Furniture Studio: The Heart of the Functional Arts, Fine Woodworking, Woodwork, Woodworker West, Woodshop News, New Mexico* magazine. Commissions: Bank of Hong Kong; Occidental Petroleum; Baird & Warner Real Estate; Temple Solel; and Congregation Israel.

LINDA M. LEVITON
Sculpture
Page 190

Linda Leviton is a full-time studio artist working in metal. She has supplemented her professional art education with additional training in blacksmithing, sheet metal construction, welding, silversmithing, patination and etching. Leviton began the Eve series five years ago. These woven wire dresses are created on a frame of heavy copper wire. These works are made life-size, then the proportions of the pieces are exaggerated, giving each piece its own personality. Recent projects: Profiled on HGTV's "Modern Masters." Commissions: Northwest Airlines, Detroit, MI; Longmont Clinics, CO; WICHE Inc., Boulder, CO; State of Ohio, Columbus Awards: Cheongju International Craft Biennale, Korea, Ohio State Fair Arts Council Award 2001. Publications: Color on Metal, 2001; Niche magazine, autumn 2001.

DANIEL LEVY
Tabletop
Page 127

Daniel Levy has been producing porcelain tableware since graduating from Alfred University in 1976 with a degree in sculpture and ceramics. He brings his fine arts background to the design of talbesettings as plates and bowls become a collage of form and color. Subtle texture, debossed surfaces and multiple layers of colored slip create pattern and imagery while 22K gold or platinum bring a visual elegance to the table. Two of Levy's dinnerware settings were exhibited in *Objects for Use* at the American Craft Museum.

JIM LICARETZ
Sculpture
Page 174

As a classically trained portrait and figure sculptor, Jim Licaretz found that there were times (while he was composing figures) that the parts were as great as the whole. Segregating portions of the completed figures gave him new direction in realizing his passion for the human form. In addition, the chance to utilize fragments as wall pieces has led to new developments in terms of materials and color. Commissions include: Claretian Seminary, Rancho Dominguez, CA; Children's Hospital, Los Angeles, CA. Collections include: Medallic sculpture at the British Museum and Smithsonian Institution. Figures and portraits include those of sculptors Richard Lippold and Peter Agostini.

BETH M. LIPPERT
Furniture
Page 80

Beth Lippert hand paints whimsical furniture. She specializes in turning ordinary furniture and everyday objects into colorful works of art that bring smiles to all who view them. These lively pieces work well in settings where they assume the starring role, but create an environment full of energy and life when used in conjunction with another piece for an office waiting room, children's play room or even a quaint sidewalk café. Lippert's work is featured in private collections across the United States and has been exhibited in solo and group shows. Prices range from $40 to $2,000.

ED MAESTRO
Sculpture
Page 208

Ed Maestro has been an artist and teacher for over 30 years, working in wood, metal and stone. His sculpture expresses the relationship and tension between beauty and anguish; beauty being expressed through the restriction of form. His skill as a fine artist and craftsman incorporates his extensive classical background as a master violinmaker and furniture designer. Maestro lived and worked in Europe for many years and still maintains a studio home in Tuscany. Maestro has exhibited widely in Europe and the U.S., including: Bruton Street Gallery, London, England; International Design, Florence, Italy; Humus Gallery, Florence, Italy; Palazzo Sani, Lucca, Italy; La Vitrine Gallery, Holland; Artrages Gallery, Amsterdam; Signature Galleries, Boston, MA; Giles and Forman, New York; Sedona Art Center, AZ; and Jamie Brice Gallery, Sedona, AZ.

ANN MALLORY
Objects
Page 163

Ann Mallory has worked in ceramics since 1971, creating one-of-a-kind vessels, sculpture, and site-specific work such as large tile tables, fountains and birdbaths. Her work is a celebration of form and the spirit inspired by nature. Pieces are contemplative, elegant and timeless, with tactile surfaces recalling ancient artifacts, bronzes, sun-baked alkaline earth or luscious fabrics like satin and velvet. All exude a sensual quality inviting to the touch. Although fired and durable, the clay has a soft quality that captures the memory of its wet, malleable origins. Collections and publications include: the Los Angeles County Museum of Art, CA; Santa Barbara Museum of Art, CA; T.W. Wood Museum, Montpelier, VT; Salzbrand International, Koblenz, Germany; *House and Garden; Elle Décor* and *Architectural Digest*. Prices begin at $800.

MARGE MARGULIES
Tabletop
Page 126

Marge Margulies has been working in Philadelphia as a professional studio potter since graduating from the Philadelphia College of Art in 1981. She exhibits her work at galleries and stores across the nation and has participated in many national craft shows. The intent of her work is to create compositions that, through the use of separate elements, give the impression of unfolding flowers. This combination of elements achieves a whole that is greater than the sum of its parts. The colorful groupings work equally well on display or in use. Each piece is wheel-thrown, then altered and painted with colored glazes. The pieces are lightweight because of Margulies' attention to throwing in an even, well-balanced way.

DALE MARHANKA
Objects
Page 162

Figural dialogue in our everyday environment is a major influence in the work of Dale Marhanka. Marhanka's intent is to produce an analogy about the balance or tension between the feminine and masculine association. These original and one-of-a-kind sculptural vessel forms are the products of the feelings, values and sensitivity the artist has actualized through clay. He has chosen the teapot, jar, vase and ewer form as the vehicles to best express this analogy and intimacy. Selected awards and exhibitions include: Individual Artist Fellowship, 2001, Virginia Commission for the Arts; San Angelo Museum of Art, 2000, San Angelo, TX; Kennedy-Douglas Center for the Arts, 1999, Florence, AL; Walter Anderson Museum of Art, 1998, Ocean Springs, MS; and the Holter Museum of Art, 1998, Helena, MT. Publications: *The Ceramic Design Book*, 1998, Lark Books. Price range: $350- $1,500.

ARTIST INFORMATION

MARK HOPKINS SCULPTURE, INC.
Sculpture
Page 179

Mark Hopkins has been sculpting professionally for over 25 years, with a style so flowing and beautiful, it is often referred to as "bronze in motion." His collector's list ranges from Clint Eastwood to Bob Hope to the Coca-Cola Corporation and many more. Hopkins' themes are as diverse as the artist himself. Some of these themes include children, western scenes and wildlife, as well as music and fishing. Sizes range from monumental to small tabletop.

MARKUSEN METAL STUDIOS LTD.
Tabletop
Page 130

Thomas Markusen has been a metal smith, designer and educator for more than 30 years and has been commissioned to create work for both the private and public sectors. His work is found in many collections, including The White House Collection of American Crafts, Washington, DC; the Vatican Museum, Vatican City, Italy; the Wustum Museum of Fine Arts, Racine, WI; and the Museum of Contemporary Crafts, New York, NY. Applying unique techniques that he has researched, developed and refined over the past 30 years, Markusen has created contemporary hollowware of the finest craftsmanship and highest aesthetic consideration for fine craft collectors. His work includes candleholders, bowls, vases, wall tondi (plates), murals and furniture. A series of limited editions combines hollowware with cast bronze.

MASAOKA GLASS DESIGN
Doors, Windows & Screens
Pages 107, 110-111

Exquisite, distinctive brilliance in stained glass. Masaoka Glass Design has been on the forefront of designing contemporary windows for 27 years. Each project is individually designed and crafted using the finest materials available to produce windows of unparalleled quality. They have installed their glass in private homes, as well as public, commercial, and liturgical buildings throughout the country. It is important to Masaoka Glass Design to work closely with the client to understand their vision so that the art represents a successful aesthetic collaboration.

MOLLIE MASSIE
Furniture
Pages 17, 71, 73

Vancouver metal artist Mollie Massie works with interior designers, architects and individual clients. Her passion is functional or "everyday art" for the home and office. Her Art to Live With line of home furnishings includes tables, fireplace screens and tools, chairs, bar stools, floor lamps and chandeliers, as well as mirror frames and cabinet pulls. Always interested in new challenges, Massie also accepts custom, site-specific jobs. She tells her clients: "The sky's the limit. If you can imagine it, I can most likely create it for you." Commissions: private homes; Grouse Mountain Resort; Vail Resort; Four Seasons Resorts; Fairmont Hotels. Publications include Metropolitan Home, Architectural Digest, Log Home Living, Log Home Design Ideas, Canadian House and Home, Style at Home, Home Magazine, Colorado Homes & Lifestyle and Better Homes and Gardens.

MICHAEL T. MAXWELL
Furniture
Page 23

Michael T. Maxwell established M.T. Maxwell Furniture Company with a commitment to preserving the art of handmade furniture while producing functional, timeless pieces for today. Maxwell's original design won the Editor's Award for New Designer at the International Contemporary Furniture Fair in 1993. Exhibits include the Philadelphia Furniture and Furnishings Show, the Washington Craft Show, the Westchester Craft Show, the Southern Highlands Craft Show and various American Craft Council shows. Maxwell's furniture is bench-made in American cherry and walnut. Custom work includes maple, bird's-eye and tiger-eye maple, walnut and mahogany. Maxwell is committed to quality, integrity and craftsmanship, while producing affordable furniture, creating a look that transcends the trends of time.

CALLAHAN McDONOUGH
Floor Coverings
Page 122

An Atlanta artist of 28 years, Callahan McDonough combines symbolic aspects of myth and spirituality with personal narrative. Her artwork has been exhibited in galleries nationally and featured in numerous publications. "The departure point for my work comes from myself, my relationships and my surroundings, but the layers of meaning that surface are always a bit of a surprise to me. I fantasize about a time when the artist and community were connected, a time when all that we celebrated and mourned was expressed in the arts." Callahan's art is inspired by collaboration with her clients – the vision they have for their lives and their environment.

McGOVNEY – CAMAROT
Tabletop
Page 135

"The creative sum is greater than the parts – our work is the best of both of us." In the seven years that Steven McGovney and Tammy Camarot have been married, they have created a body of artwork that draws on each other's strengths. His sculpture and ceramic background provides reference for the three-dimensional and technical side, while her intuitive sense of pattern helps design the tableware's two-dimensional surfaces. McGovney designs and slip casts each piece in low-fire white clay, hand finishing it with pulled spouts, handles and sculptural additions. After the first firing, Camarot gains control, painting underglaze colors and delicately scribing highlights. Fired again, the piece is dipped in a clear glaze and sent to the kiln one last time.

ELIZABETH RYLAND MEARS
Sculpture
Page 200

Elizabeth Ryland Mears is a full-time, award-winning studio artist. She creates works in glass and mixed media primarily using the glassblowing technique known as flamework. Whether created representationally or conceptually, all of the work reflects her strong connection with nature and cyclical time. Mears has studied repeatedly at Penland, Pilchuck and Corning. She has twice received Niche Awards, as well as awards in national exhibits, for her creations. Her glass creations have been included in numerous national and international exhibitions on the art of glass and the art of flameworked glass. Her book, Basic Flameworking, is scheduled for publication in spring 2003. Her work is represented in galleries throughout North America and is included in many private collections.

JUDY MINER
Architectural Details
Page 103

Judy Miner received her B.A. and M.A. in ceramics from the University of Louisville and has been working in clay for 20 years. She has created custom architectural installations from Hawaii to Kentucky, including sinks, tile and cabinet pulls. The calm, organic beauty of her art reflects her life and work along the banks of the Ohio River. Each piece is handmade in porcelain and fired by Miner, who ensures that every piece is unique to your project. Miner's extraordinary functional art for daily living is based on her belief that function creates a dialogue between the user and the object, thus creating a relationship between the user and the maker.

ARTIST INFORMATION

MARILYN MINTER
Objects
Page 155

Marilyn Minter received her B.A. in ceramics from the Kansas City Art Institute. Her work has received many awards in the Washington, DC, area. Minter has completed commissions for profit and non-profit organizations in the DC area. Her work has been purchased by collectors from all over the world; one such purchase was given as a gift to a Buddhist Temple in Japan. Her designs range from structured, plaid pots to those that are completely abstract. Her abstract designs are created somewhat subconsciously while she watches TV and relaxes with a scotch. The firing offers the final surprise: a unique work of art, rich in design and color.

WILLIAM AND RENEE MORRIS
Lighting
Page 89

William and Renee Morris handcraft lamps of hardwood and mica by allowing natural beauty to dictate final form. William Morris uses only select fine woods, including mahogany and fallen redwood, in handcrafting each base. Renee Morris accents art shades with hand-collected leaves and hand-cut motifs. Together they create table, desk and floor lamps, which radiate elegance and quality in corporate and private settings. Commissions include: Edmonds Community College Library, Lynnwood, WA. Awards include: The Rosen Group's Niche Award, 1997 and 1996.

ANDREW MUGGLETON
Furniture
Page 33

Andrew Muggleton combines extraordinary woods with metal and glass to create furnishings with spare, elegant lines. Dining room tables and chairs, console tables, beds, entertainment units and sets of drawers have been crafted with a nod to comfort and an eye towards beauty. Simplicity is a hallmark of Muggleton's design. He notes that keeping his design simple—avoiding the trap of filling empty space with unnecessary clutter—is one of his hardest and most rewarding challenges. Several of his designs are so innovative that he has patents on them. Muggleton's exhibitions include Best of Show at the Boulder Arts Festival, CO; Sculpture, Objects and Functional Art (SOFA), Chicago, IL; and Furniture on the Park, Denver, CO. Publications include *Architecture & Design of the West, Fine Woodworking* magazine and *Northern Home* magazine.

TOM NEUGEBAUER
Garden Sculpture
Page 217

Tom Neugebauer has been creating sculptures in both clay and metal since the 1970s. Widely exhibited and collected, his work is known for its unique combination of materials. The artist frequently draws inspiration from the human form with sweeping, dance-like movement. *At the Center*, an abstract series including *The Welcome*, features dynamic, interwoven "arms" of various metals that embrace and support a central clay sphere. In his *Hop, Skip and a Jump* series of life-sized outdoor sculptures, he explores the exuberant world of children's games. The scale generally ranges from three to ten feet high, making his pieces suitable for the home, landscape, office or public setting. He also welcomes site-specific or large-scale commissions. Corporate collections: Bankers Trust, Delta Airlines, Chubb, Marsh Company and Wyeth.

JAMES NOWAK
Objects
Page 139

Artist James Nowak studied at the Pilchuck Glass School. His work is representative of the powerful Seattle-based glass movement. Having worked with many of the region's finest glass blowers, and through continued education and experimentation, Nowak has maintained his creative edge for over two decades. His work covers a broad spectrum of design capabilities, from custom lighting designs to cast glass walls and unique interior accessories. Nowak says of his work: "My designs express a renaissance in glass art." Mingling classical techniques with current technologies, he produces objects that play with color and light for the contemporary viewer.

SUSAN M. OAKS
Objects
Page 166

Susan M. Oaks, a longtime artist, has exhibited nationally and internationally in places such as Chicago, Los Angeles, New York City and Belize City, Belize. She has won numerous awards. Her one-of-a-kind coiled vessel forms are made from wool, silk, linen and cotton, and consist of a variety of shapes, sizes, textures and colors. Beyond these formalist elements, she uses her medium to express thoughts, feelings and emotions, creating on a conceptual level. She has been awarded grants from the Texas Commission on the Arts and the National Endowment for the Arts. Oaks regularly presents slide lectures, sharing the history of her creative art vessels at universities, museums and art groups. The vessels range in price from $150 to $950. Information regarding prices, slides and lectures is available on request.

MASUO OJIMA
Objects
Page 165

Masuo Ojima's work represents his personality and character. Purity of form and subtlety are his foundation. Because he has lived in the U.S. for more than half of his life, it is inevitable that his work should be influenced by western culture, philosophy and style. However, his inner thoughts are strongly rooted in eastern culture and religion. A free spirit must exist to make his work alive and to communicate with others.

VINCENT LEON OLMSTED
Sculpture
Pages 201, 221

"My work deals with the complex reality of the medium of glass as a home for the human psyche." Vincent Leon Olmsted is a storyteller. A found object housed within each of his glass works serves as the central starting point of his narrative and lures us into the chronicle of each piece. Figurative drawing engraved on the surface details the course of the story. Pouring molten glass into a sand mold, Olmsted contrasts the natural seductiveness of polished glass with the rough surface of cast glass. Illustrating his ideas most recently with the forms of the figure and the house, he allows us to view inside each piece, into the perplexing center of his visual fiction. Awards: Wisconsin Arts Board fellowship, CitiArts grant.

SAM OSTROFF
Furniture
Page 74

The sculpture of emerging artist Sam Ostroff engages the viewer and encourages interaction. Working in a nineteenth-century New England mill, Ostroff has built an extensive body of mostly functional sculpture—some of which is meant to serve a greater purpose—all with the same vision. Working primarily in steel, his technique is a fusion of Nouveau-era blacksmithing and contemporary metal fabrication methods. His style, often described as dramatic and theatrical, draws on design elements from the Art Nouveau movement and the Machine Age. Shapes fashioned by Hector Guimard and Victor Horta—and later revisited by Albert Paley—often reveal their influence in Ostroff's work. The influence of decorative artists, combined with an expressionistic sensibility, puts Sam Ostroff's work into a category of its own.

ARTIST INFORMATION

BEN OWEN III
Objects
Pages 148-149

"It is my goal to honor my past while creating my own artistic path in clay, all the while remembering my grandfather's advice: 'Keep it simple, son. Keep it simple.'" Ben Owen III continues a pottery tradition in clay that dates back to colonial America. He studied under his grandfather, Ben Owen, Sr., and received his B.F.A. in ceramics from East Carolina University. Ben specializes in wood-fired vessels with a contemporary touch. His handmade pottery reflects refined traditional forms featuring signature glazes in vibrant reds, rich jade greens and subtle earth tones. Selected exhibitions and collections: Lill Street Gallery, Chicago, IL; Pinch Gallery, Northhampton, MA; Mint Museum of Craft and Design, Charlotte, NC; Chrysler Museum, Norfolk, VA; Elton John and Bob Hope.

ANNIE PASIKOV
Sculpture
Page 192

A dozen years ago, after teaching art for twenty years (including eleven while living at a residential school for troubled teens), Annie Pasikov responded to a health crisis by giving wings to her passion for creating. She began doing art instead of just assisting others with their creativity. After lifelong interest, she taught herself to sculpt in stone. Her gracefully flowing forms emerge through a direct approach sketching on the stones, often without the use of maquettes. Pasikov listens to the whisper of intuition that seems to guide her as she considers her design: a unique dance between art sense and sixth sense. It is deeply satisfying to see hearts touched by the sculptures, with seventeen sales recently at two weekend exhibitions. More information and photos are available upon request.

PETER PIEROBON
Furniture
Page 34

Peter Pierobon studied with the eminent American furniture designer, Wendell Castle, and has maintained his own studio since 1985. Unlike many contemporary furniture makers, his inspiration has come largely from the world of fine art and sculpture. Seeking to establish a fresh relationship between the primitive and the sophisticated while maintaining respect for the craft tradition, Pierobon strives to infuse his work with new possibilities. He has been granted many awards and his work has been collected by museums and individuals internationally, including the Renwick Gallery, the American Craft Museum, the Philadelphia Museum of Art and the Mint Museum. He is excited about the possibility of working with clients and solving specific needs in a creative and stimulating manner. Prices range from $5,000 to $40,000.

EMI OZAWA
Objects
Page 156

Emi Ozawa creates sculptural objects and toys primarily in wood. Her focus is on the box and how it can be opened and closed, not what it could contain. The shape of the box develops as she explores ways of opening it. By combining geometric shapes, bright colors and moving parts, Ozawa evokes the simple pleasure of playing with an object. She attended the Rhode Island School of Design and received an M.F.A. in furniture design in 1992. Exhibitions: *Contemporary Studio Case Furniture: The Inside Story*, 2002, Elvehjem Museum of Art, Madison, WI; *Celebrating Boxes*, 2001, United Kingdom; *Joshibi: A Centenary Exhibition*, 2000, Japan. Awards: Honorable Mention, 1999, American Craft Council, Baltimore Market. Publications: *Object Lessons*, 2001; *Furniture Studio: The Heart of the Functional Art*, 1999.

PECK TILE, POTTERY & SCULPTURE
Furniture
Page 52

For over 20 years, Leo Peck has created unique and imaginative ceramic art. He began his career as a functional potter and soon transitioned into custom tile and sculptural ceramics. Highlights of his work include ceramic tables and commissioned projects. Peck's craftsmanship is superb. Instead of broken tile, he creates tile from his custom clay. Tile edges are smoothed and cleaned before firing. His fun table designs reflect his adventurous spirit. Glazes range from lively and vibrant to simple and complementary. Constructed on steel and concrete, his durable tables are also suitable for outdoors. Peck's custom work has been incorporated into a variety of commercial and residential projects, including pools, fireplaces, kitchens, bathrooms, waterfalls and restaurants. To explore Leo Peck's work, please visit www.pecktile.com.

PINKWATER GLASS
Sculpture
Page 203

Glass artists Lisa Schwartz and Kurt Swanson combine their design and humor to skillfully create glasswork in the unmistakably unique style that has made Pinkwater Glass renown across the country. Known for its lyrical style and unusual sense of color, Pinkwater Glass has been sold in galleries and museum shops in the U.S. and Europe. Over the past 20 years, Pinkwater Glass has garnered numerous awards from the art world and accolades from the popular press. Their work is included in the permanent collections of the American Craft Museum, the Renwick Museum and the White House. Currently, Schwartz and Swanson are designing sculpture, lighting, furniture and other startlingly beautiful glass installations for private and corporate collections.

PAM MORRIS DESIGN EXCITING LIGHTING
Lighting
Pages 85,131

Pam Morris, owner of Exciting Lighting, is a distinguished design innovator. Her clients encompass top restaurants, hotels and private collectors, including Wolfgang Puck, Sugar Ray Leonard, Georgio Armani and the Hong Kong Regent Hotel. "In my work, I create highly original and evocative illuminated pieces. I use light, together with blown, slumped or cast glass and forged or cast metal, to create art pieces that reflect a special sense of place." Morris' work has been featured in previous GUILD sourcebooks.

BINH PHO
Objects
Page 157

Binh Pho is Chicago based artist who works primarily with wood, combining lathe work, sculpting, piercing and gilding techniques to create commanding, primitive art forms. His work has received numerous awards and has been collected internationally. Museum, public and corporate collections include: The White House, Washington DC; Arrowmont School of Art and Craft, Gatlinburg TN; and Honeywell, Cupertino, CA. Exhibitions include: SOFA, New York, NY and Chicago, IL; *Branching Out: Contemporary Wood Turning in 2002*, Ellipse Arts Center, Arlington, VA, and coinciding with *Wood Turning in North America since 1930*, Renwick Gallery of the Smithsonian American Art Museum, Washington, DC. Pho is internationally known as demonstrator and is a faculty member at Tennessee Technological University and the Arrowmont School of Art and Craft.

DEAN PULVER
Furniture
Page 35

Dean Pulver's ideas begin with rough sketches. The creative impulses, however, continue through the whole process, and changes can occur at any time. This interaction with the piece gives it a life of its own. "My interests lie in building pieces that have presence, vitality and life." Pulver usually chooses one of his favorite woods to carve, walnut or mahogany. Using the band saw and power carvers, he roughs out the forms, then uses traditional carving tools to define the images or designs. One of his main interests in furniture making is drawing from various cultures' design aesthetics. "Most recently I have been involved in designing and making pieces that have a similar spirit as primitive art. I admire the innocence and honesty within this work and hope to speak in a similar voice."

ARTIST INFORMATION

MAYA RADOCZY
Doors, Windows & Screens
Page 109

Maya Radoczy is known for creating cast glass collages, bas-relief images and sculpture for corporate, public and residential projects. She exhibits internationally and is included in numerous collections. Commissions: Elliot Hotel, 2001, Seattle, WA; REI Flagship Stores, 2000, Tokyo, Japan, and Denver, CO; King St. Center, 1999, Seattle, WA; Deschutes County Library, 1999, Bend, OR. Exhibitions: International Sculpture Invitational, 2001, Seadrift, TX; Sculpture show, 2000, Erlangen, Germany; *Northwest Women in Glass*, 1999, Tacoma, WA; *Focus on Fire: Fine Art in Architecture*, Seattle, WA, 1994. Publications: *Glass House*, 2002; *Seattle Homes & Lifestyles* magazine, 2001, "Modern Masters," HGTV, 1999.

LYNN EVERETT READ
Objects
Page 138

Lynn Everett Read works with glass much like a weaver works with thread; textiles and fabrics influence much of his work. The majority of Read's work is created using blown-glass techniques, and he often incorporates ancient techniques such as canne, murrine or incalmo. These processes allow the artist to create imagery and pattern out of glass strings and glass sheets. His work is exhibited nationally and prices range from $200 to $2,400. Commissioned works range from $1,000 to $40,000. Private commissions include: Hugh and Ann Bynum, 2002, Portland, OR; Jeff Weddle, Portland, OR; and Chris Jaffe, 2000, Yarrow Point, WA. Corporate commissions include: Lisa Bradford Salon, 2000, Portland, OR; Savoy Studios, Portland, OR; Loca Noche Restaurant, 2001, New York, NY; and Imus Coffee Shop, 2001, Mohegan Sun, CT.

RED FERN GLASS
Lighting
Page 90

Ed Pennebaker creates glass lighting for the home, office and public space. He seeks to take advantage of the luminous quality of transparency inherent to glass. Light coming from within and reflecting off the surface of the glass reveals pattern and texture. The individual pieces work as a group and function as a chorus of forms. Sizes range from 16" to 10' or larger. Prices start at $950. Exhibitions of his work include: Hsinchu International Art Glass Festival, 2001, Taiwan; *A Glass Act*, Prism Contemporary Glass, 2001 and 2000, Pontiac, MI; *Hot & Cool*, traveling exhibit of contemporary glass, 2000-2001, various venues. He is the recipient of the following awards: Best of Show, 2002 Invitational, Little Rock Convention Center, AR; Excellence in Lighting Award, Philadelphia Furniture & Furnishings Show, 2002, PA.

RIVERSIDE ARTISANS
Furniture
Page 30

Riverside Artisans has built on the principle of "following your bliss," says founder Jim Galileo. A move in 2002 brought Riverside Artisans to a shop in a historic building in downtown Paterson, New Jersey. Defining a style that embraces curves and flowing shapes while maintaining balance and weight has helped keep Riverside Artisans satisfying high-end residential customers. Kelly Pierce chose Riverside Artisans for inclusion in his acclaimed book, *The Custom Furniture Sourcebook*, published by Taunton Press in 2000. Close, personal attention is a hallmark of the Riverside Artisans design philosophy. Design is always viewed as the coming together of beauty, function and the personality of the client. Together Jim Galileo and his son, Aaron, infuse their business with a respect and love for the work, their clients and each other.

ROB FISHER SCULPTURE
Sculpture
Page 193

Fabricated in stainless steel and aluminum, the artwork of Rob Fisher ranges in scale from floor and wall pieces, such as Chambered Nautilus, for private residences, to the Arrivals Hall of the Philadelphia International Airport. Commissions: monumental kinetic sculpture, 2002, Gateway Exchange, Columbia, MD, aluminum masts, stainless steel nets and rigging, and painted aluminum; suspended atrium sculpture, 2003, National Education Association headquarters, Washington, DC, painted steel, anodized aluminum and stainless steel; Ark Door sculpture and Eternal Light, 2002, Temple Beth El, Lancaster, PA, bronze and copper; aerial sculpture, visitor center, 2002, AstraZeneca Pharmaceuticals, Wilmington, DE. Fisher's work has been featured in previous GUILD sourcebooks.

KEVIN B. ROBB
Garden Sculpture
Page 218

Kevin Robb creates individual contemporary sculptures in stainless steel or bronze, as well as limited-edition cast bronze for intimate environments or large-scale public areas. Robb brings a natural curiosity to his work, combined with the understanding of how positive and negative spaces, shadow and light work together. Recent Projects: Pueblo Community College, CO; Frederick Meijer Gardens, Grand Rapids, MI; Marchon Corporate Headquarters, Melville, NY. Commissions: Premier, Inc., Charlotte, NC; Lake Isle Townhome, East Chester, NY.

236

ROBERT CALDWELL, DESIGNER AND CRAFTSMAN
Furniture
Page 22

Robert Caldwell likes to refer to his work as contemporary furniture in the arts and crafts tradition. He is comfortable with traditional forms but not doctrinaire. Most of his work is done in solid hardwoods. Caldwell graduated from Rice University in 1974 and spent several years in outpatient psychiatric social work before turning to cabinet making in 1983. Nearly everything he knows about the fine points of woodworking was learned from Mr. Ian Kirby at summer seminars in Atlanta, GA, in the mid-1980s. He currently shows his work at American Craft Council fairs throughout the United States. Recently his focus has been on creating chairs and bending wood, but he also enjoys learning new methods of work. His prices range from $400 to $3,000.

JAMIE ROBERTSON
Furniture
Pages 44-45

Jamie Robertson has been making one-of-a-kind and limited-edition furniture since 1972. His work is in numerous private collections throughout the country and has been exhibited in a wide variety of galleries and museums, including the California Crafts Museum and the Society of Arts & Crafts in Boston. In 1976 Robertson built a new "figurehead" for the *USS Constitution* and in the mid-1990s, he presented his first one-person show at Pritam & Eames Gallery. His work has been featured in numerous publications, including *American Craft, Art New England* and *Object Lessons*, 2001. His awards for design and craftsmanship include the Niche First Prize and the Dairy Barn's Excellence in Craftsmanship Award. More important than all of these credentials, perhaps, is the fact that people simply want his work.

ROCK COTTAGE GLASSWORKS, INC.
Lighting
Page 84

Rock Cottage Glassworks, Inc. creates hand-blown and cast glass objects and combines them with wrought iron, wood or stone to produce custom lighting. All items are available for commission. Please view their website at www.vankeppelartglass.com for extensive lighting commissions.

ARTIST INFORMATION

ALAN ROSEN
Furniture
Page 65

Since 1974, Alan Rosen has been creating distinctive original and custom furniture known for its simple elegance, uncompromising craftsmanship and attention to detail. The careful selection of woods, traditional joinery and signature hand-rubbed finish ensure enjoyment by future generations. Commissions: William Gates III, 1999, Medina, WA; Paul Allen, 1999, Mercer Island, WA; David Usher, 1995, Carmel, CA; Sacred Heart Church, 1993, Bellevue, WA. Collections: Grizzly Industrial Inc., Bellingham, WA, Columbus, MD, and Williamsport, PA.

ROSETTA
Garden Sculpture
Pages 209, 212

Rosetta's art training comes from the University of Delaware, the Art Center College of Design in Los Angeles, CA, and a 20-year career in graphic design. A fellow in the National Sculpture Society and a member of the Society of Animal Artists, she has won awards from both of these organizations, as well as Bennington Center for the Arts, Pen & Brush, Allied Artists of America and the Bosque Conservatory of Art. Rosetta's sculptures can be seen at the Lincoln Park Zoo in Chicago, IL; Chapman University, Orange, CA; Alden Vineyards, Healdsburg, CA, and in the cities of Loveland, CO; Lakewood, CO; Dowagiac, MI; Champaign-Urbana, IL, and Brownwood, TX. She has exhibited widely in group and solo shows both in the U.S. and abroad and has work in private, corporate and museum collections.

JAMES T. RUSSELL
Garden Sculpture
Page 216

Elegantly crafted and fastidiously polished, James T. Russell's sculptures are ribbons of stainless steel, gracefully arching and twirling in space. His professional career is in its fourth decade and includes worldwide commissions of innovative and durable sculptures ranging from wall reliefs to gallery pieces to fountain installations and monumental towers. Prices range from $3,200 to $300,000. Collections and commissions include the Motorola headquarters in Beijing, China; Architectural Digest; Princess Cruise Line ships; and the City of South San Francisco, CA.

FRANK J. SANTOVIZ, JR.
Architectural Details
Page 106

Frank J. Santoviz, Jr. takes tremendous pride in creating architectural pieces that blur the boundaries between art, furniture and interior elements, such as bathroom vanities and kitchens. Santoviz believes that every element of a building, either residential or commercial, can be recreated as a work of art or sculpture. Functionality is the key component to all his designs. To create these contemporary designs, Santoviz combines a variety of materials, including aluminum, stainless steel, marble, granite, glass, wood and Dupont Corian. Combining materials gives each piece texture and depth and allows it to accent virtually any environment. Santoviz fabricates both his own designs as well as commissioned pieces.

LOIS S. SATTLER
Objects
Page 154

Lois Sattler has been involved with clay for many years. Formally a painter, she uses the clay as her canvas. Her work is handbuilt and each piece is one-of-a-kind. The majority of her work is done in porcelain, though she also works with a black fired clay. Ms. Sattler's work can be seen in decorator showrooms and galleries, as well as museum gift shops. She is also involved with teaching children through the STAR enrichment program, which has been honored by the Clinton White House and the U.S. Department of Education.

SCAVENGER FURNITURE ART, LLC
Furniture
Page 49

Scavenger Furniture Art evolved from Mark Orr's appreciation of antique architectural elements. Scavenger pieces combine the old with the new — antique shutters, for instance, become tabletops or the sides of cabinets, and old stair balusters become table legs. Larger cabinets have tops made of old tin ceiling and drawers with porcelain doorknobs as pulls. Ornamentation includes antique locks and keys, mosaic work and often a hand-carved basswood raven, the symbol of Scavenger Art. The end result is a whimsical line of sculptural and functional furniture that appeals to people of all ages and walks of life. Orr's work is carried in arts and crafts galleries across the country and has been featured in *The Philadelphia Inquirer, The Detroit News* and *Scratching the Surface*, 2002.

DUTCH SCHULZE
Objects
Page 142

Dutch Schulze has been blowing glass for 15 years and is best known for his glass vessels, evocative in design and rich in color. These large vases and fluted bowls can be found in fine homes and galleries throughout the country. Schulze is a versatile artist who began his career as a sculptor 30 years ago. He continues this work in cast glass and specializes in representational relief sculptures. His latest commission was a 15 x 11 foot suspended steel and cast glass sculpture for Texas Tech University in Amarillo, TX. Commissions and collections: Health Sciences Center, Texas Tech University, Amarillo; Toyota Corporation, Japan; Sprint Corporate Collection, Reston, VA; William Treston Associates, Houston, TX; Nordstrom Department Stores, Seattle, WA; John Warner Kluge, Palm Springs, FL; Bart Starr, professional football player, Detroit, MI.

SEYMOUR L. SHUREN
Sculpture
Page 181

Seymour Shuren's creative sculptures have appeared in galleries, museums and art society exhibitions and are owned by many private collectors. The diversity of his subject matter and materials create an enhanced environment for any artistic or decorative setting. One of the many natural wonders of nature is the formation of a multitude of stones in various colors, shapes and densities. As a sculptor he attempts to uncover the chromatic beauty of alabaster and marble by creating a representative and/or amorphous shape that will elicit an aesthetic, emotional response from both the artist and the observer. The resulting sculptures not only speak to us as forms in space, but radiate with the natural colors of nature's own extensive palette. Prices range from $2,000 - $15,000.

GERALD SICILIANO
Sculpture
Page 175

Gerald Siciliano is pleased to present a new limited-edition sculpture series in bronze, stainless steel and terra cotta. Attractively priced, these elegant and enduring works are offered in a range of finishes and sizes to enhance any collection or setting. Siciliano's classical and traditionally based figurative and non-representational sculptures are meticulously crafted to the highest standards for discerning collectors worldwide. He invites your inquiries via telephone, email or the Internet. Clients and collections: American Airlines; American Axle & Manufacturing Company; Bristol-Myers Squibb Company; The Brooklyn Museum; Canon USA; Chang-Won Provincial Government Sculpture Park, Korea; Dong Baek Art Center, Korea; The John Templeton Foundation; and private collectors worldwide.

ARTIST INFORMATION

JOSH SIMPSON
Objects
Pages 144-145

For over 30 years, Josh Simpson has been using age-old techniques in creating hand-blown glass at his studio in the foothills of the Berkshire Mountains in western Massachusetts. Simpson's glass sculptures are celebrated nationally and internationally for their extraordinary, complex beauty. His dream-like landscapes of the seas, the skies and the heavens are compelling and enigmatic. They are also technical feats without parallel. Collections: Josh Simpson Sphere Museum, Japan; Corning Museum of Glass, NY; Mint Museum, NC; Brunnier Museum, IA; Museum of Fine Arts, Boston, MA; Museum of Decorative Arts, Prague; Chrysler Museum, VA; and the Renwick Gallery, Smithsonian Institution, Washington, DC. Commissions: American for the Arts, NY; Royal Caribbean Cruise Lines, Norway; Museum of Modern Art, NY; and the Earth Day Awards, NY.

LISA SLOVIS
Tabletop
Page 133

Lisa Slovis is a metalsmith whose work includes jewelry, Judaica and objects for the home. Her work allows her to thematically combine two important areas of her life: athletics and art. By incorporating movement and function in these pieces, the participant is enticed to interact with them on a more intimate and tactile level. Developed using characteristics of toys and traditional ceremonial objects, these pieces can be used for practical purposes or play. Slovis creates serious yet whimsical pieces using sterling silver or pewter, with accents in brass, bronze and nickel. She received her M.F.A. from San Diego State in 1998 and her B.F.A. from the University of Wisconsin-Madison in 1995. She exhibits at shows across the country, teaches workshops and also does custom work.

KIMBERLY SOTELO
Furniture
Page 61

Kimberly Sotelo redefines willow furniture, bringing it into a contemporary setting in both design and function. Using this familiar material, Sotelo transforms the coldness of modern design into something warm and inviting. She creates a hybrid of something modern that nonetheless reverberates with the past. Through the use of careful selection, repetition and thoughtful design, Sotelo is able to create movement within these highly functional pieces. Each piece takes on its own voice and is the result of a conversation between the artist and the willow. The work is refined and elegant, yet peaceful and comforting. It reminds us that in today's society, even as our perceptions of aesthetics change, we still need continual contact with nature.

GARY SLATER
Garden Sculpture
Page 215

Gary Slater's trademark metal is hand-textured copper, which is combined with smooth copper or polished stainless steel. Geometric forms are the building blocks from which he combines a wide variety of sculptures, from garden size to monumental installations, with or without water. Having worked in direct metal sculpture for over 32 years, Slater has become a master in his craft. Commissions include: Chase Manhattan Bank, Tempe, AZ; Stetson University, Deland, FL; Center Park II, Calverton, MD; Scottsdale Center for the Arts, Scottsdale, AZ; Dawn Princess Cruise Ship; City of Phoenix, AZ; University of Minnesota-Minneapolis.

BRAD SMITH
Furniture
Page 29

Brad Smith's furniture incorporates the new and the old. Born in 1954 and raised on a farm in Pennsylvania, Smith learned that nothing should be wasted. While studying at the Rochester Institute of Technology, he developed this idea into his design aesthetic. Since 1980 Smith has given old lumber a new life, whether in a chest of drawers or an armoire: pitchforks become the backs of benches and chairs, and ax handles are the legs for stools. The blend of new wood, salvaged barn boards, ax handles and pitchforks all combine to create the distinctive "Bradford look." Smith produces a small line of furniture, which can be seen throughout the country. Each year he also produces a number of one-of-a-kind pieces on speculation and commission.

STRINI ART GLASS
Tabletop
Pages 125, 128-129

Rick Strini creates handblown glass, made without the use of molds to achieve the desired shape. He molds and shapes the glass by hand; the design and functionality of each piece evolves naturally. Strini uses the Italian method of glassmaking, working at the bench with hot glass, but without assistance. This is Strini's 38th year in glass and it is his career of choice. He works in his private studio and displays museum pieces in his private showroom in downtown Santa Cruz, CA. His current work reflects his lifelong fascination with the ocean and everything below it. The colors, shapes and forms of these *Reefscapes* reflect the living ocean and its inhabitants. Sea baskets, clams, sea fans, jellyfish and seahorses are just a few of the creatures that are combined with the vibrant colors of the glass.

SLEDD/WINGER GLASSWORKS
Doors, Windows & Screens
Page 117

Since 1985 Nancy Sledd and Mary Lu Winger have collaborated in a multifaceted stained glass studio, featuring internationally collected commission work as well as limited-production gallery pieces. Known for their meticulous attention to detail, this versatile pair works closely with clients to determine design and color direction. Often combining such divergent elements as fiber optics, water and fusing, Sledd and Winger constantly strive for the unexpected. Projects range from entryways and windows to furniture, lighting and sculpture. Exhibits and awards: American Craft Council (ACC) Spotlight; Baltimore ACC; Philadelphia Furniture Show; Smithsonian Craft Show; numerous *Niche* magazine awards. Publications: *Niche* magazine, *Stained Glass Basics, Glass Craftsman, Stained Glass for the First Time, Glass Art, Home & Design, Leadlight.*

PHILIP S. SOLLMAN
Furniture
Page 5, 27

The extraordinary organic quality of Phil Sollman's work has been included in dozens of publications, featured in a special public television production and recognized for its originality through a grant from the National Endowment for the Arts and a fellowship from the Pennsylvania Council on the Arts. Using his own design, Sollman has been creating furniture from indigenous woods for more than 30 years. Exceptional comfort, graceful lines and uniquely original forms characterize the quality of his furniture. Sollman's background in architecture enables him to easily visualize your individual space. He will be receptive to your needs and straightforward with his advice. He will always welcome your inquiries. A color brochure and complete resume are available upon request.

STUDIO PARAN
Objects
Page 143

Studio Paran is the creative endeavor of Richard Jones. The studio was founded in 1989 with a commitment to producing handblown glass characterized by strong design, skilled craftsmanship, bold use of color and innovative form. Through the years, Jones has continued to develop the Paran line, expanding its range and scope while holding to the hallmarks of solid design and fine craftsmanship. He has recently developed a technique for encasing detailed images in glass and uses this technology to create limited-edition pieces, in addition to the studio's production lines. The glasswork of Studio Paran can be found in galleries, museum shops and fine retailers across the country.

ARTIST INFORMATION

JOHN SUTTMAN
Furniture
Page 48

Beautiful and unusual, classical to contemporary, John Suttman's metal furniture and decorative iron-work is designed and built like nothing else. Updating architectural and design motifs from earlier periods, he translates classic objects – previously crafted in marble or wood – to steel. The finishes are luxurious, with rich patinas that evoke rare and precious artifacts or sleek, modern machinery. Suttman has a growing portfolio of standard and limited-edition furniture. He will also build custom furniture or architectural elements such as gates, railings or lighting to your specific requirements.

TRIO DESIGN GLASSWARE
Architectural Details
Page 101

Contemporary designs and bold colors exemplify Renato Foti's work. His main focus is to add structure, balance, color and simplicity to home and work environments. Balance is of critical importance to the designed spaces; it is a reflection of Foti's personal philosophy in life and in his art. These fused and slumped glass products range from small coasters to very large decorative wall sculptures, panels and sinks. Exhibitions: *One of a Kind*, 2001, Chicago, IL; *Retro Material Matters*, 2001, Toronto, ON; *The Masks We Wear*, 1998, Sandra Ainsley Gallery and Sculpture Society of Canada, Toronto, ON. Publications: *Canadian House & Home*, Dec/Jan, 2001-2002; *Glass Craftsman*, 2000.

CINDY VARGAS
Furniture
Page 43

Cindy Vargas is a furniture artist and woodworker. She received her training at the Oregon College of Art and Craft and the University of Minnesota with degrees in the fine arts and concentrations in woodworking, furniture design and fiber arts. She often combines wood with hand-dyed, hand-printed textiles to create one-of-a-kind sculptural furniture. Using themes such as music and dance, or taking her inspiration from the natural world, she builds colorful and animated pieces. Vargas has been the recipient of a grant through the Craft Alliance of New York State and an award for emerging artists by the Lake Oswego Craft and Art League, among others. She has also taught classes in woodworking and furniture painting. Her work has been exhibited nationally.

JANET TORELLI
Tabletop
Page 132

Janet Torelli, a self-taught sterling tableware designer, draws her unique designs from architectural and organic forms. While some have found the influence of fine jewelry in her designs, Torelli sees her work as a marriage of functionality and contemporary elegance for the table. She resides in Chicago, which provides a fertile source for design ideas. Prices for these hand-crafted items range from $85 to $275. Her designs include hors d'oeuvre picks, serving tongs, dessert servers and cocktail accessories. There are three series: *Ornato*, which is inspired by vintage wrought iron; *Organica*, which centers around a natural theme; and *Luxe*, which embraces pure opulence. She has been published in many national magazines, and her designs have appeared on the NBC show "Friends." Torelli is a member of the American Craft Council.

TUSKA INC.
Doors, Windows & Screens
Page 112

Tuska Inc. represents the work of fine artist John R. Tuska (1931-1998). The studio offers reproductions of one of the artist's most engaging works: *Illuminates*, cutworks of the human form engaged in the motion of dance, suspended on open screens. Each screen is assembled by hand to order in custom dimensions and materials, ranging from natural materials such as woods, steel, aluminum or bronze to contemporary polymers. Each screen is meticulously executed and rendered in exceeding detail. True craftsman quality makes them ideal for use as window or wall hangings, room dividers, gates, shutters, landscape decorations or other custom applications.

MARK A. WALLIS
Sculpture
Page 191

Visual poetry. Wood constructions embodying fine craftsmanship with aesthetic compositions designed to offer viewers a point of reflection. All sculptures designed and built by the artist incorporating a variety of exotic and domestic woods and accented with paint, graphite and/or stone.

LUIS TORRUELLA
Garden Sculpture
Page 219

Puerto Rican sculptor Luis Torruella designs in a contemporary, abstract context. His Caribbean heritage is reflected in his work's color, rhythm and movement. Torruella collaborates with architects, designers and developers in public and private commissions. Collections: Museo de Arte de Puerto Rico, San Juan; Mead Art Museum, Amherst, MA; Performing Arts Center, San Juan, PR; Skokie Sculpture Park, IL. Exhibitions: Palma de Mallorca, 2001, Spain; Galeria Botello, 2002, 1997, 1994, 1992, San Juan, PR; Theatrical Institute, 1992, Moscow, Russia; World Expo, 1992, Seville, Spain; and numerous private exhibitions. Torruella's work has been featured in previous GUILD sourcebooks.

JOËL URRUTY
Sculpture
Page 195

Joël Urruty received his M.F.A. in woodworking from the School of American Crafts at the Rochester Institute of Technology in 1996. He creates unique wood sculpture for the home and office. His work has been exhibited nationally and internationally in galleries and museums. He has won several awards and has been included in various art publications. His abstract figurative sculptures range from tabletop sizes to larger floor pieces. Prices start at $1,100.

DICK WEISS
Doors, Windows & Screens
Pages 116, 118-119

Dick Weiss received a B.A. from Yale University in 1968. He has worked in stained glass since 1971. For the past ten years, his focus has been on leaded glass windows using hand-blown glass called rondels. These flattened discs contain incredible life. Each is unique. The rondels are blown by some of the finest North-west glassblowers: Ben Moore, Katherine Gray, Preston Singletary, Sonja Blomdahl, Dante Marioni and Paul Cunningham. Whether the glass is clear or colored, the leaded panels will glow in virtually any kind of light. Awards include two National Endowments for the Arts grants and two Hauberg Fellowships at the Pilchuck Glass School. Public commissions include the Seattle-Tacoma International Airport, WA; the McConnell Foundation, Redding, CA, and the General Dynamics Corporation, Falls Church, VA (with Sonja Blomdahl).

ARTIST INFORMATION

JAY WHYTE
Furniture
Page 67

After 10 years as a very unsatisfied electrician, Jay Whyte can happily say that he is now a self-taught woodworker and sculptor of six years. His passion for the craft has driven him to squeeze as much time as he can out of every day, learning something new in woodworking. From a young age, he has always had a strong desire to work with his hands and be creative, and woodworking gives him that opportunity. Whyte goes to great lengths to search for the most beautifully figured woods available, after which he uses many conventional and unconventional methods to bring his pieces to a rough shape. He then proceeds to the refinement stage, where he uses an angle grinder and several specialty sanders to bring the pieces into final form. Whyte's work is collected nationwide and is currently on display in many of the nation's top art galleries.

JOHN WESLEY WILLIAMS
Furniture
Page 28

John Wesley Williams produced his first piece of furniture 27 years ago and during that time, he has discovered that a true sense of accomplishment comes from building and learning. If he could sustain that, his work and life would be honest and alive. All of his pieces are built from the ground up. This gives each one a natural aesthetic as it rises from the dusty shop floor. The final result is enhanced by a pure oil finish that invites you to touch. This tactility is taken to an extreme in his Gaudiesque scalloped pieces. All works are solid hardwoods, not veneers, impeccably finished, front and back. Work this demanding deserves an equally enduring design beyond fads and foibles.

ERIK A. WOLKEN
Furniture
Page 42

Erik Wolken seeks to create furniture that is both personal and animated. He creates unique, functional pieces using simple organic shapes, wood and paint. Wolken has been building furniture on a professional basis for the past 15 years and has been exhibiting his work nationwide through shows and galleries for the last seven years. He won an emerging artist grant from the Durham, North Carolina, Arts Council in 1997, has twice been awarded scholarships to study at Anderson Ranch and has been published in *American Craft* magazine and *Object Lessons: Beauty and Meaning in Art*.

DAVID WOODRUFF
Objects
Page 164

David Woodruff creates one-of-a-kind hollow-formed vessels and other art objects from woods that possess great character as a result of trauma in the growing environment. This combination of genetic and environmental forces provides the raw materials for the multidimensional beauty found in Woodruff's art objects. The artist, using a wood lathe and museum-quality lacquer, creates art pieces that reveal the beauty of the variety in nature. Commissions: Weaver-Cooke Construction, Greensboro, NC; Novant Healthcare, Winston-Salem, NC. Exhibitions and Awards: top score, Krasl Art Fair, St. Joseph, MI; top score, Tennessee Association of Craft Artists Crafts Fair, Chattanooga, TN; Piedmont Craftsman Guild, NC; Ann Arbor Street Fair, MI. Woodruff's work has been featured in previous GUILD sourcebooks.

ZEN STONE FURNISHINGS
Furniture
Pages 82, 161

Cleo and Sol Hill met, married and started creating beautiful objects together in 1997. Their union is called Zen Stone Furnishings, and their mission is to create functional art objects that create sacred spaces in our daily lives by bringing the beauty of nature indoors. Their lamps are made out of salt cedar and local river stones. The lampshades are made out of handmade papers collected from all over the world. Furniture pieces are made out of copper-plated metal, with salt cedar legs and stone tops. Sol and Cleo work out of their studio in Santa Fe, NM (with the help of two assistants) and own a gallery downtown. Prices range from $300-$630 for the lamps and $700-$9,000 for the furniture pieces. Lampshades are sold separately. Cleo and Sol enjoy working with clients to create custom furnishings.

LARRY ZGODA
Doors, Windows & Screens
Pages 6, 108

Larry Zgoda has been an artist of stained glass for nearly 30 years. Designs that reflect the essence of place, material innovations and a reflective consideration of the total environment root Larry Zgoda's stained glass installations prominently in the architectural ornament tradition. Recent projects: Our Lady of the Angels Chapel, Marian Village Retirement Community, Lockport, IL. Commissions: Woodfin Suites, Emeryville, CA; TCF Tower, Minneapolis, MN; AARP, Washington, DC. Publications: *The Art of Stained Glass*, 1998; *Beautiful Things*, 2000; *Stained Glass Quarterly*, Fall 2001. Zgoda's work has also been featured in previous GUILD sourcebooks.

ZUERNER DESIGN LLC
Furniture
Page 31

Zuerner Design LLC creates simple, elegant wood furniture and furnishings. Peter Zuerner is a designer and self-taught furniture artist. His current line emphasizes the natural grain, color and special features of New England hardwoods such as cherry, maple and walnut. Simple lines and gentle curves create pleasing and functional works of art. Zuerner's love for the material shows in the occasional special knot, unusual grain or bark edge – details that make every piece unique. He takes pride in making very comfortable furniture that will last for generations. His work is personal and passionate, his designs classic in their simplicity. Because each piece of furniture is custom made to order, individual specifications can be met. Custom designs are always considered.

A LIST OF FAVORITE GALLERIES

Each year, the publisher of *AmericanStyle* and *Niche* magazines asks artists to name favorite galleries.
The following list is based on responses from a poll of more than 26,000 artists in North America.

Thanks to the Rosen Group for permission to reprint the list. To order subscriptions to *Niche* or *AmericanStyle*, call 800-272-3893.

A Mano Gallery
128 S Main Street
New Hope, PA 18938
215-862-5122

Abacus
44 Exchange Street
Portland, ME 04101
207-772-4880

Accipiter
2046 Clark Avenue
Raleigh, NC 27605
919-755-9309

Agora Arts
104 East Water Street #1
Decorah, IA 52101
563-382-9584

American Artisan
4231 Harding Road
Nashville, TN 37205
615-298-4691

American Craft Gallery
163 South Street
Morristown, NJ 07960
973-538-6720

An American Craftsman
1866 Route 284, PO Box 480
Slate Hill, NY 10973
845-355-2400

Animazing Gallery
461 Broome Street
New York, NY 10013
212-226-7374

Annapolis Pottery
40 State Circle
Annapolis, MD 21401
410-268-6153

ArtCraft Collection
8600 Foundry Street
Savage, MD 20763
410-880-4863

Artful Hand Gallery
36 Copley Place
Boston, MA 02116
617-262-9601

Artique
161 Lexington Green Circle
Lexington, KY 40503
859-272-8802

Artisan Center
2757 East 3rd Avenue
Denver, CO 80206
303-333-1201

Artisans Gallery
Box 133 Shop #35
Peddlers Village
Lahaska, PA 18931
215-794-3112

Arts & Artisans Ltd
36 South Wabash Suite # 604
Chicago, IL 60603
312-855-9220

Arts Company
125 North Townville Street
Seneca, SC 29678
864-882-0840

As Kindred Spirits
1611 Rockville Pike 1206
Rockville, MD 20852
301-984-0102

Bluestem Missouri Crafts
13 South Ninth Street
Columbia, MO 65201
573-442-0211

BNOX Iron & Gold
404 First Street
PO Box 156
Pepin, WI 54759
715-442-2201

Browning Artworks Ltd
Highway 12
PO Box 275
Frisco, NC 27936-0275
252-995-5538

By Hand South
112 East Ponce de Leon Avenue
Decatur, GA 30030
404-378-0118

Cambridge Artist Cooperative
59A Church Street
Cambridge, MA 02138
617-868-5966

Campbell Pottery Store
25579 Plank Road, PO Box 246
Cambridge Springs, PA 16403
814-734-8800

Capitol Craftsman
16 North Main Street
Concord, NH 03301
603-224-6166

CBL Fine Art
459 Pleasant Valley Way
West Orange, NJ 07052
973-736-7776

Citywoods
651 Central Avenue
Highland Park, IL 60035
847-432-9393

Clarksville Pottery Galleries
4001 N Lamar Blvd #200
Austin, TX 78756
512-454-8930

Clay Pot
162 7th Avenue
Brooklyn, NY 11215
718-788-6564

Craft Company No. 6
785 University Avenue
Rochester, NY 14607
716-473-3413

Creations Fine Woodworking Gallery
451 Hockessin Corner
Hockessin, DE 19707
302-235-2310

Dashka Roth Jewelry & Judaica
332 Chartres Street
New Orleans, LA 70130
504-523-0805

Dennison-Moran Gallery
696 5th Avenue South
Naples, FL 34102
941-263-0590

241

Designers Studio
492 Broadway
Saratoga Springs, NY 12866
518-584-1977

Dickinson & Wait Craft Gallery
121 E German Street
PO Box 1273
Shepherdstown, WV 25443
304-876-0657

Don Drumm Studios & Gallery
457 Crouse Street
Akron, OH 44311
330-253-6268

Don Muller Gallery
40 Main Street
Northampton, MA 01060
413-586-1119

DreamWeaver
364 St. Armands Circle
Sarasota, FL 34236
941-388-1974

Dunn Mehler Gallery
337 Mirada Road
Half Moon Bay, CA 94019
650-726-7667

Earthenworks Gallery
713 First Street
PO Box 702
La Conner, WA 98257
360-466-4422

Edgecomb Potters Galleries
727 Boothbay Road
Edgecomb, ME 04556
207-882-9493

Edgewood Orchard Galleries
4140 Peninsula Players Road
Fish Creek, WI 54212
920-868-3579

Eureka Crafts
210 Walton Street
Syracuse, NY 13210
315-471-4601

Evergreen Contemporary Crafts
291 Main Street
Great Barrington, MA 01230
413-528-0511

Fabrile Gallery
224 South Michigan Avenue
Chicago, IL 60604
312-427-1510

Fire Opal
320 Harvard Street
Brookline, MA 02446
617-739-9066

Fireworks Gallery
210 First Avenue South
Seattle, WA 98104
206-682-8707

Freehand Fine Crafts
8413 West Third Street
Los Angeles, CA 90048
323-655-2607

Gallery 3-2-1
65 W State Street, Box 369
Oxford, NY 13830
607-843-9538

Gallery Of The Mountains
290 Macon Avenue, PO Box 8283
Asheville, NC 28804
828-254-2068

Gifted Hand
32 Church Street
Wellesley, MA 02482
781-235-7171

Glass Reunions of Key West
825 Duval Street
Key West, FL 33040
305-294-1720

Good Goods Gallery
106 Mason Street
Saugatuck, MI 49453
616-857-1557

Grovewood Gallery
111 Grovewood Road
Asheville, NC 28804
828-253-7651

Handworks Gallery
161 Great Road
Acton, MA 01720
978-263-1707

Hanson Galleries
800 W. Sam Houston Pkwy N. # E118
Houston, TX 77024
713-984-1242

Heart of the Home
28 South Main Street
New Hope, PA 18938
215-862-1880

Heart to Heart Gallery
921 Ridge Road
Munster, IN 46321
219-836-2300

Imagine Artwear
1124 King Street
Alexandria, VA 22314
703-548-1461

Island Style
2075 Periwinkle #16
Sanibel Island, FL 33957
941-472-6657

Kebanu
4-1354 Kuhio Highway #3
Kapaa Kauai, HI 96746
808-823-6820

Lazar's Art Gallery
2940 Woodlawn Avenue NW
Canton, OH 44708
330-477-8351

Left Bank Gallery
25 Commercial Street
PO Box 764
Wellfleet, MA 02667
508-349-9451

Limited Editions
2200 Long Beach Blvd.
Surf City, NJ 08008
609-494-0527

Log House Craft Gallery
Berea College
Berea, KY 40404
859-985-3226

Luma
1 Lake Avenue
PO Box 1439
Colorado Springs, CO 80901
719-577-5835

Mackerel Sky Gallery
217 Ann Street
East Lansing, MI 48823
517-351-2211

Mind's Eye Craft Gallery
201 South Talbot Street
PO Box 781
St. Michaels, MD 21663
410-745-2023

Moondance Gallery
603 Meadowmont Village Circle
Chapel Hill, NC 27517
919-7265-0020

Mostly Clay & Fine Crafts
227 Broad Street
Nevada City, CA 95959
530-265-3535

Mountain Laurel Crafts
1 North Washington Street
PO Box 369
Berkeley Springs, WV 25411
304-258-1919

NJM Gallery
8 Bow Street
Portsmouth, NH 03801
603-433-4120

Nan Gunnett & Co.
25 Briarcrest Square
Hershey, PA 17033
717-533-1464

Nancy Markoe Fine
American Crafts Gallery
3112 Pass A Grille Way
St. Pete Beach, FL 33706
727-360-0729

Ocean Annie's
815 A Ocean Trail
Corolla, NC 27927
252-453-4102

Patina Gallery
131 West Palace Avenue
Santa Fe, NM 87501
505-986-3432

Pismo Gallery
235 Fillmore Street
Denver, CO 80206
303-333-2879

Primavera
4 Bowen's Wharf
Newport, RI 02840
401-841-0757

Purple Sage
110 Don Gaspar
Santa Fe, NM 87501
505-984-0600

RAF
5 West York Street
Savannah, GA 31401
912-447-8807

Raiford Gallery
1169 Canton Street
Roswell, GA 30075
770-645-2050

Rasberry's Art Glass Gallery
6540 Washington Street
Yountville, CA 94599
707-944-9211

Sansar
4805 Bethesda Avenue
Bethesda, MD 20814
301-652-8676

Seekers Glass Gallery
4090 Burton Drive
PO Box 521
Cambria, CA 93428
800-841-5250

Seldom Seen
817 East Las Olas Boulevard
Ft. Lauderdale, FL 33301
954-764-5590

Selo/Shevel Gallery
301 South Main Street
Ann Arbor, MI 48104
734-761-4620

Shapiro's
185 Second Avenue North
St. Petersburg, FL 33701-0714
727-894-2111

Show of Hands
210 Clayton Street
Denver, CO 80206
303-399-0201

Signature Stores
10 Steeple Street
Box 2307
Mashpee, MA 02649
508-539-0029

Snyderman Gallery/Works Gallery
303 Cherry Street
Philadelphia, PA 19106
215-922-7775

Society of Arts and Crafts
175 Newbury Street
Boston, MA 02116
617-266-1810

Stone's Throw Gallery
1389 Beacon Street
Brookline, MA 02146
617-731-3773

Stowe Craft Gallery
55 Mountain Road
Stowe, VT 05672
802-253-4693

Studio 41
700 First Street
Benicia, CA 94510
707-745-0254

Surprises
4003 Westheimer
Houston, TX 77027
713-877-1900

Topeo Gallery
35 North Main Street
New Hope, PA 18938
215-862-2750

Vault
1339 Pacfic Avenue
Santa Cruz, CA 95060
831-426-3349

Village Artisans Gallery
321 Walnut Street, PO Box 303
Boiling Springs, PA 17007
717-258-3256

Wild Goose Chase
1431 Beacon Street
Brookline, MA 02446
617-738-8020

Wood Merchant
707 South First Street
La Conner, WA 98257
360-466-4741

ZYZYX!
10301 A Old Georgetown Road
Bethesda, MD 20814
301-493-0297

GLOSSARY OF ART TERMS

Alabaster
George Westbrook, turned vessel with wood rim.
Photograph: William Thus.

Beading
Linda Fifield, *Fire Lizards II*.
Photograph: Jack Fifield.

Celadon
Janice Rowell, *Fractal Platter*.
Photograph: Dana Davis.

China Paint
Rimas VisGirda, *Flower Vase*.
Photograph: Rimas VisGirda.

ACRYLIC	A water-soluble paint made with pigments and synthetic resin; used as a fast-drying alternative to oil paint.
ALABASTER	A fine-textured, usually white, gypsum that is easily carved and translucent when thin.
ALUMINUM	A lightweight, silver-colored metal used extensively in commercial applications, and occasionally by metal artists. In a process called "anodizing," aluminum is given a tough, porous coating that can be colored with dyes.
APPLIQUÉ	A technique whereby pieces of fabric are layered on top of one another and joined with decorative stitches.
BAS-RELIEF	Literally, "low-relief." Raised or indented sculptural patterns that remain close to the surface plane.
BATIK	A method of applying dye to cloth that is covered, in part, with a dye-resistant, removable substance such as wax. After dyeing, the resist is removed, and the design appears in the original color against the newly colored background.
BEADING	The process whereby decorative beads are sewn, glued or otherwise attached to a surface.
BEVELED GLASS	Plate glass that has its perimeter ground and polished at an angle.
BONDED GLASS	Glass pieces that have been adhered together by glue, resin or cement.
BRASS	An alloy of copper and zinc. Brass is yellow in color, and though harder than either of its constituents, it is appropriately malleable for jewelry making.
BRONZE	Traditionally, an alloy of copper and tin widely used in casting. The term is often applied to brown-colored brasses.
BURL	A dome-shaped growth on the trunk of a tree. Intricately patterned burl wool is often used by wood turners and furniture makers.
CASTING	The process of pouring molten metal or glass, clay slip, etc. into a hollow mold to harden. Some casting processes permit more than one reproduction.
CELADON	French name for a green, gray-green, blue-green or gray glaze produced with a small percentage of iron as the colorant.
CERAMICS	The art and science of forming objects from earth materials containing or combined with silica; the objects are then heated to at least 1300°F to harden.
CHASING	A technique in which steel punches are used to decorate and/or texture a metal surface.
CHINA PAINT	A low-temperature overglaze fired onto previously glazed and fired ceramic.
DICHROIC GLASS	A thin metallic coating on any type of glass. The coating is applied at a high temperature in a vacuum chamber.
DIE FORMING	The process of placing metal between two steel dies or stamps and squeezing them together under high pressure. This process shapes and strengthens the metal.
DIPTYCH	Artwork on two panels that are hung together. Historically, a hinged, two-paneled painting or bas-relief.

GLOSSARY OF ART TERMS

EARTHENWARE Ceramic ware with a permeable or porous body after firing (usually to a temperature of 1600°F to 1900°F).

EMBOSSING A decorative technique in which a design is raised in relief.

ENAMELED GLASS Glass decorated with particles of translucent glass or glass-like material, usually of a contrasting color, which fuses to the surface under heat. Multicolored designs can be created, as well as monochrome coatings.

ENAMELS As applied to metals: a transparent or opaque glaze that melts at a lower temperature than copper, silver or gold, on which enamel is used as the decorative finish; usually fired to about 1300°F.

ETCHED GLASS Glass decorated, carved or otherwise marked by sandblasting or the use of hydrofluoric acid. The glass is partially covered with an acid-resistant wax or gum and the exposed area is etched.

EXTRUSION The process of shaping plastic clay by forcing it through an auger or form.

FIRING Heating clay, glaze, enamel or other material to the temperature necessary to achieve a desired structural change. Most ceramics are fired in a kiln to temperatures ranging from 1600°F to 2300°F.

FORGED A blacksmithing technique in which metal is shaped by hammering, usually while at red or white heat.

FUMING A vapor deposition process in which a thin film of metal (usually silver, platinum or gold) condenses on the surface of a hot piece of glass or clay, resulting in an iridescent surface.

FUSED GLASS Glass that has been heated in a kiln to the point where two separate pieces are permanently joined as one without losing their individual color.

GLASSBLOWING The process of gathering molten glass onto the end of a blowpipe and forming it into a variety of shapes by blowing and manipulating it as the glass is rotated.

GLAZE Glassy melted coating on a clay surface. Glaze has a similar oxide composition to glass, but includes a binder.

GREENWARE Unfired clay objects.

HUE The pure state of any color.

INCALMO The glassblowing technique used to create horizontal or vertical bands of color by forming and connecting cylinders of colored glass.

INCLUSIONS Particles of metal, bubbles, etc., that occur naturally within glass or are added for decorative effect.

INLAY A decorating technique in which an object is incised with a design, a colorant is pressed into the incisions, and the surface is then scraped to confine the colored inlay to the incisions.

INTAGLIO A printmaking process in which an image is created from ink held in the incised or bitten areas of a metal plate, below the surface plane. Engraving, etching, mezzotint and aquatint are examples of the intaglio process.

IRIDIZED GLASS Flat or blown glass sprayed with a vapor deposit of metal oxides for an iridescent finish. The iridized layer, which resembles an oil slick, can be selectively removed for a two-tone effect.

Earthenware
Kathryn Berd, cup and saucer.

Forged
Lisa Jacobs, steel barstools.
Photograph: Bob Barrett.

Fused
Robert Hoke and Therese Nolan,
Etch Totem.

Incalmo
Sam Stang, three-band glass bowl.

GLOSSARY OF TERMS

Lampwork
Katherine Gray, candelabra.

Luster Glaze
Gail McCarthy, vase.
Photograph: Photographics Two.

Mosaic
Eileen Jager, table fountain with inlaid glass.
Photograph: Tommy Olof Elder.

Porcelain
Michael Lambert, *Struttin' Teapot.*
Courtesy of Ferrin Gallery.

KILN	A furnace for firing clay, forming glass or melting enamels; studio kilns can achieve temperatures up to 2500°F and can be fueled with gas, wood or electricity.
KILN-FORMING	A glass-forming process that utilizes a kiln to heat glass in a refractory or heat-resistant mold, slump glass over a form, or fuse two or more pieces of glass together.
KINETIC	Active. Kinetic sculpture has parts that move, whether by air currents (as with a mobile) or by motors and gears.
LAMINATED	Composed of layers bonded together for strength, thickness or decorative effect.
LAMPWORK	The technique of manipulating glass by heating it with a small flame. An open flame is advantageous in very detailed work.
LEADED GLASS	Glass containing a percentage of lead oxide, which increases its density and improves its ability to refract and disperse light. Leaded glass is used for ornaments and for decorative and luxury tableware.
LIMITED EDITION	Artworks produced in a deliberately limited quantity. All items in the edition are identical and each one is an original work of art. The limited size of the edition enhances the value of each piece.
LINOCUT	A relief print process similar to woodcut. Wood blocks covered with a layer of linoleum are carved with woodcut tools, coated with ink and printed by hand or in a press.
LOW-FIRE GLAZES	Low-temperature ceramic glazes, usually associated with bright, shiny colors.
LUSTER	A brilliant iridescent film used on ceramic glazes; formed from metallic salts.
MAJOLICA	An opaque glaze, usually white, with a glossy surface. Typically decorated with bright overglaze stains.
MARQUETRY	Decorative patterns formed when thin layers of wood (and sometimes other materials, such as ivory) are inlaid into the surface of furniture or other wood products.
MOSAIC	The process of creating a design or picture using small pieces of glass, stone, terra cotta, etc.
MURRINI	A small wafer of glass bearing a colored pattern. Formed by bundling and fusing colored glass rods together and then heating and pulling the resulting cylinder to a very small diameter. When cut into cross-sectioned wafers, each piece bears the original pattern in miniature.
PASTEL	A crayon of ground pigment bound with gum or oil. Pastel crayons have varying ratios of pigment to chalk and gum; the more pigment, the more intense the color.
PATE DE VERRE	A "paste" of finely crushed glass that is mixed, heated and poured into a mold.
PATINA	A surface coloring, usually brown or green, produced by the oxidation of bronze, copper or other metal. Patinas occur naturally and are also produced artificially for decorative effect.
PORCELAIN	A clay body that is white, strong and hard when fired. When sufficiently thin, it is also translucent.

GLOSSARY OF TERMS

RAKU
: The technique of rapidly firing low-temperature ceramic ware. Raku firings were used traditionally in Japan to make bowls for tea ceremonies.

REPOUSSÉ
: An ancient process in which sheet metal is hammered into contours from both the front and the back.

SALT GLAZE
: A glaze created during high-temperature firings. Sodium, usually in the form of rock salt, is introduced into the fully heated kiln and forms a clear coating on the clay, often with an orange-peel texture.

SAND CASTING
: An ancient and still widely used casting method in which moistened sand is packed against a model to make a mold.

SANDBLASTING
: A method of etching the surface of a material by spraying it with compressed air and sand.

SEPIA
: Warm, reddish-brown pigment produced from octopus or cuttlefish ink, used in watercolor and drawing ink. In photography, some toning processes produce a similar color in the print.

SLUMPED GLASS
: Preformed flat or three-dimensional glass that is reheated and shaped in a mold.

SPALTED
: Wood that contains areas of natural decay, giving it distinctive markings. Spalted wood is used for its decorative effect.

STILL LIFE
: A depiction of a group of inanimate objects arranged for symbolic or aesthetic effect.

STONEWARE
: A gray-, reddish- or buff-colored opaque clay body that matures (becomes nonporous) between 1900°F and 2300°F.

TERRA COTTA
: Low-fired ceramic ware that is often reddish and unglazed.

TERRA SIGILLATA
: A thin coating of colored clay or clays applied like a glaze. A terra sigillata solution is composed of fine particles of decanted clay and water.

TRIPTYCH
: A three-paneled artwork. Historically, triptychs were hinged together so that the two side wings closed over the central panel.

TROMPE L'OEIL
: Literally, "fool the eye" (French). An object or scene rendered so realistically that the viewer believes he or she is seeing the real thing.

TURNED
: Wood or other materials shaped by tools while revolving around a fixed axis, usually a lathe. Cylindrical forms (dowels, rungs) and circular designs (bowls) are made in this way.

VITREOUS
: Clay fired to maturity, so that it is hard, dense and nonabsorbent.

WHITEWARE
: A generic term for white clay bodies.

WOODCUT
: A relief printing process in which a picture or design is cut in relief along the grain of a wood block.

WROUGHT
: Shaped by beating or hammering, often elaborately, for decorative effect. "Wrought iron" is a low-carbon metal that can be elongated without breaking and is resistant to corrosion.

Raku
Candone Wharton, *Atlas III*.
Photograph: Seth Tice-Lewis.

Spalted
Phil Brown, turned wood vessel.

Stoneware
Cathi Jefferson, *Olive Pit Dish*.

Turned
Christian Burchard, *Baskets, Three Parts*.
Photograph: Rob Jaffe.

ACKNOWLEDGMENTS

This book could not have been completed without the
collaboration and support of the entire team at GUILD
Sourcebooks, especially Toni Sikes who birthed the idea
in the first place. GUILD's enthusiasm for the concept and
ongoing commitment to the celebration of art in all of its
forms made this project very meaningful. Katie Kazan,
you are so devoted and simply amazing. Special thanks to
the customers of GUILD who shared their artful homes
and stories with me, particularly Bobbie Seril in New York.
Most affectionately, thanks to Estelle Ellis, a wise friend,
for her insights; Mary Drysdale, whose work speaks with
such eloquence; Michael Strohl, for his promotional support;
and my kids, Sophie and Jacob, who remind me every day
that living with art is a family affair.

—Louis Sagar

Special artwork for special places.

Furniture, Sculpture & Objects is one of two volumes in the *Artful Home* series. We invite you to purchase the companion volume, *Art for the Wall*, available now.

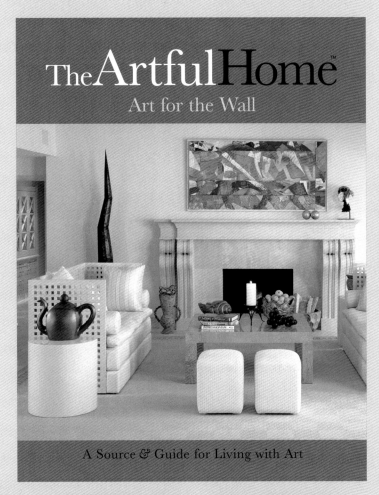

- Paintings
- Photographs
- Prints
- Ceramic Tiles and Wall Reliefs
- Murals and Painted Finishes
- Art Quilts
- Tapestry, Fiber and Paper
- Mixed and Other Media

The Artful Home: Art for the Wall

248 pages   412 color photographs

Beautiful artworks for a beautiful home $29.95

Call 1-877-284-8453 to order your copy now.

GUILD SOURCEBOOKS

GEOGRAPHIC INDEX

250

GEOGRAPHIC INDEX

INDEX OF ARTISTS & COMPANIES

INDEX OF ARTISTS & COMPANIES